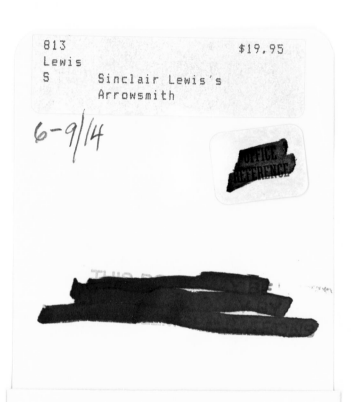

Modern Critical Interpretations
Sinclair Lewis's
Arrowsmith

Modern Critical Interpretations

These and other titles in preparation

Modern Critical Interpretations

Sinclair Lewis's

Arrowsmith

Edited and with an introduction by
Harold Bloom
Sterling Professor of the Humanities
Yale University

Chelsea House Publishers ◊ *1988*
NEW YORK ◊ NEW HAVEN ◊ PHILADELPHIA

Printed and bound in the United States of America

10 9 8 7 6 5 4 3 2 1

∞ The paper used in this publication meets the minimum
requirements of the American National Standard for Permanence
of Paper for Printed Library Materials, Z39.48–1984.

Library of Congress Cataloging-in-Publication Data
Sinclair Lewis's Arrowsmith / edited and with an introduction by
    Harold Bloom.
        p. cm.—(Modern critical interpretations)
    Bibliography: p.
    Includes index.
    Summary: A selection of critical essays on Lewis's novel
scrutinizing the medical profession.
    ISBN 1-55546-046-1 (alk. paper): $19.95
    1. Lewis, Sinclair, 1885–1951. Arrowsmith. [1. Lewis,
Sinclair, 1885–1951. Arrowsmith. 2. American literature—
History and criticism.] I. Bloom, Harold. II. Series.
PS3523.E94A86   1988   87–30680
                                                       CIP
                                                        AC

Contents

Editor's Note

This book gathers together a representative selection of the best critical interpretations of Sinclair Lewis's novel *Arrowsmith*. The critical essays are reprinted here in the chronological order of their original publication. I am grateful to Anna Carew and Carol Clay for their assistance in editing this volume.

My introduction reads *Arrowsmith* as a romance of science with allegorical overtones, but finds an unintentional irony in the novel's concluding tone. Frederic I. Carpenter begins the chronological sequence of criticism with an overview of Lewis's work as an involuntary saga of idealism's defeat by American reality.

In Charles E. Rosenberg's discussion, Arrowsmith's fate is seen as being overdetermined both by "Lewis's desire to depict greatness and his inability to conceive of its being allowed to exist within American society."

Marilyn Morgan Helleberg rather severely questions the strength of Lewis's characterizations, while Lyon N. Richardson studies the genesis of the novel and the process of revision that it then underwent. A sympathetic analysis by Martin Light finds the weaknesses of *Arrowsmith* to be the result of Lewis's own deep ambivalences towards the literary mode of romance.

Mary G. Land compares Lewis to Theodore Dreiser, reading both *Arrowsmith* and *An American Tragedy* by the after-illumination provided by Walker Percy's *Love in the Ruins*. In this volume's closing essay, Robert L. Coard studies the role of Sherlock Holmes in Lewis's depiction of Max Gottlieb, Martin Arrowsmith's scientific ego ideal and role model.

Introduction

It cannot be said, thirty-five years after his death, that Sinclair Lewis is forgotten or ignored, yet clearly his reputation has declined considerably. *Arrowsmith* (1925) is still a widely read novel, particularly among the young, but *Main Street* (1920) and *Babbitt* (1922) seem to be best known for their titles, while *Elmer Gantry* (1927) and *Dodsworth* (1929) are remembered in their movie versions. Rereading *Main Street* and *Elmer Gantry* has disappointed me, but *Babbitt* and *Dodsworth,* both good novels, deserve more readers than they now seem to have. Lewis is of very nearly no interest whatsoever to American literary critics of my own generation and younger, so that it seems likely his decline in renown will continue.

A Nobel prizewinner, like John Steinbeck, Lewis resembles Steinbeck only in that regard, and is now being eclipsed by Faulkner, Hemingway, Fitzgerald, and such older contemporaries as Cather and Dreiser. Lewis venerated Dickens, but the critical age when Lewis's achievement could be compared to that of Dickens or of Balzac is long ago over. Hamlin Garland, an actual precursor, is necessarily far more comparable to Lewis than Dickens or Balzac are. If, as Baudelaire may have remarked, every janitor in Balzac is a genius, then every genius in Lewis is something of a janitor. Essentially a satirist with a camera-eye, Lewis was a master neither of narrative nor of characterization. And his satire, curiously affectionate at its base (quite loving towards Babbitt), has no edge in the contemporary United States, where reality is frequently too outrageous for any literary satire to be possible.

Lewis has considerable historical interest, aside from the winning qualities of *Babbitt* and the surprising *Dodsworth,* but he is likely to survive because of his least characteristic, most idealistic novel, *Arrowsmith.* A morality tale, with a medical research scientist as hero, *Arrow-*

1

smith has enough mythic force to compel a young reader to an idealism of her or his own. Critics have found in *Arrowsmith* Lewis's version of the idealism of Emerson and Thoreau, pitched lower in Lewis, who had no transcendental yearnings. The native strain in our literature that emanated out from Emerson into Whitman and Thoreau appears also in *Arrowsmith,* and helps account for the novel's continued relevance as American myth.

II

H. L. Mencken, who greatly admired *Arrowsmith,* upon expectedly ideological grounds, still caught the flaw in the hero and the aesthetic virtue in the splendid villain, Pickerbaugh:

> Pickerbaugh exists everywhere, in almost every American town. He is the quack who flings himself melodramatically upon measles, chicken pox, whooping cough—the organizer of Health Weeks and author of prophylactic, Kiwanian slogans—the hero of clean-up campaigns—the scientific beau ideal of newspaper reporters, Y.M.C.A. secretaries, and the pastors of suburban churches. He has been leering at the novelists of America for years, and yet Lewis and De Kruif were the first to see and hail him. They have made an almost epic figure of him. He is the Babbit of this book—far more charming than Arrowsmith himself, and far more real. Arrowsmith fails in one important particular: he is not typical, he is not a good American. I daresay that many a reader, following his struggles with the seekers for "practical" results, will sympathize frankly with the latter. After all, it is not American to prefer honor to honors; no man, pursuing that folly, could ever hope to be president of the United States. Pickerbaugh will cause no such lifting of eyebrows. Like Babbitt, he will be recognized instantly and enjoyed innocently. Within six weeks, I suspect, every health officer in America will be receiving letters denouncing him as a Pickerbaugh. Thus nature imitates art.

Mencken's irony has been denuded by time; Arrowsmith is indeed not typical, not a good American, not a persuasive representation of a person. Neither is anyone else in the novel a convincing mimesis of actuality; that was hardly Lewis's strength, which resided in satiric caricature. *Arrowsmith* ought to be more a satire than a novel, but unfortunately its hero is an idealized self-portrait of Sinclair Lewis. Idealization of science, and of the pure scientist—Arrowsmith and his mentor, Gottlieb—is what most dates the novel. I myself first read it in 1945, when I was a student at the Bronx High School of Science, then an abominable institution of the highest and most narrow academic standards. As a nonscientist, I found myself surrounded by a swarm of hostile and aggressive fellow-students, most of whom have become successful Babbitts of medicine, physics, and related disciplines. *Arrowsmith,* with its naive exaltation of science as a pure quest for truth, had a kind of biblical status in that high school, and so I read it with subdued loathing. Rereading it now, I find a puzzled affection to be my principal reaction, but I doubt the aesthetic basis for my current attitude.

Though sadly dated, *Arrowsmith* is too eccentric a work to be judged a period piece. It is a romance, with allegorical overtones, but a romance in which everything is literalized, a romance of science, as it were, rather than a science fiction. Its hero, much battered, does not learn much; he simply becomes increasingly more abrupt and stubborn, and votes with his feet whenever marriages, institutions, and other societal forms begin to menace his pure quest for scientific research. In the romance's pastoral conclusion, Arrowsmith retreats to the woods, a Thoreau pursuing the exact mechanism of the action of quinine derivatives. Romance depends upon a curious blend of wholeheartedness and sophistication in its author, and Sinclair Lewis was not Edmund Spenser:

> His mathematics and physical chemistry were now as sound as Terry's, his indifference to publicity and to flowery hangings as great, his industry as fanatical, his ingenuity in devising new apparatus at least comparable, and his imagination far more swift. He had less ease but more passion. He hurled out hypotheses like sparks. He began, incredulously, to comprehend his freedom. He would yet determine the essential nature of phage; and as he became stronger and surer—and no doubt less human—he saw ahead of him innumerable inquiries into chemotherapy and immunity; enough adventures to keep him busy for decades.
>
> It seemed to him that this was the first spring he had ever seen and tasted. He learned to dive into the lake, though the

first plunge was an agony of fiery cold. They fished before breakfast, they supped at a table under the oaks, they tramped twenty miles on end, they had bluejays and squirrels for interested neighbors; and when they had worked all night, they came out to find serene dawn lifting across the sleeping lake.

Martin felt sun-soaked and deep of chest, and always he hummed.

I do not believe that this could sustain commentary of any kind. It is competent romance writing, of the Boy's Own Book variety, but cries out for the corrected American version as carried through by Nathanael West in *A Cool Million* and in *Miss Lonelyhearts*. West's Shrike would be capable of annihilating salvation through back to nature and pure research by promising: "You feel sun-soaked, and deep of chest, and always you hum."

Arrowsmith was published in the same year as *The Great Gatsby* and *An American Tragedy*, which was hardly Lewis's fault, but now seems his lasting misfortune. *Babbitt* came out the same year as *Ulysses*, while *Dodsworth* confronted *The Sound and the Fury*. None of this is fair, but the agonistic element in literature is immemorial. *Arrowsmith* is memorable now because it is a monument to another American lost illusion, the idealism of pure science, or the search for a truth that could transcend the pragmatics of American existence. It is a fitting irony that the satirist Sinclair Lewis should be remembered now for this idealizing romance.

Sinclair Lewis and the Fortress of Reality

Frederic I. Carpenter

During the decade of the 1920s the novels of Sinclair Lewis achieved an acclaim unequaled in the history of American literature. First *Main Street,* then *Babbitt* and *Arrowsmith* appealed to popular imagination and to critical judgment alike, each selling hundreds of thousands of copies. By general agreement Sinclair Lewis became spokesman of a new renaissance in American writing, and finally won world recognition with the first award to an American of the Nobel Prize for literature, in 1930. No such immediate success, combining the popular and the critical, the national and the international, has fallen to the lot of any American, before or since. As recently as August 5, 1944, the distinguished contributors to the *Saturday Review of Literature* for the past twenty years voted *Arrowsmith* the most important novel of the period.

But following the award of the Nobel Prize in 1930, the reputation of Sinclair Lewis steadily declined. By popular and critical agreement, his novels written after then became progressively worse. As literary fashions shifted from realism to symbolism, and popular attitudes from individualism to conservatism, critics began to ask: "How Good Is Sinclair Lewis?" In 1948 Warren Beck denounced the 1930 award of the Nobel Prize as "outrageous." And Bernard DeVoto accused Lewis of defaming the American character, calling the conception of *Arrowsmith* itself "romantic, sentimental, and, above all, trivial." Increasingly, even Lewis's admirers began to wonder: Why

From *College English* 16, no. 7 (April 1955). © 1955 by the National Council of Teachers of English.

had his later novels become so bad? Had his earlier novels ever really been so good? Once again they saw illustrated in his career the fate of "the artist in America." For, beyond any possible question, Sinclair Lewis had been the representative American artist of his era.

In his Stockholm address on receiving the Nobel Prize, Lewis had described "the American novelist" as working "alone, in confusion, unassisted save by his own integrity." And the words accurately described Lewis himself. The confusion of values in which he worked may explain both his successes and his failures. When he was able to describe this confusion objectively, as in *Babbitt,* or to project his own integrity in a character such as that of *Arrowsmith,* he approached greatness. But as he grew older he found himself progressively involved in the confusion. The representative American artist progressively failed to understand, and so to transcend the confusion of his society.

The confusion of values which Lewis imputed to American society, and which he himself shared, is suggested by a sentence from one of his last (and worst) novels. *The God-Seeker,* published in 1949, told of a young missionary to the Sioux Indians in 1850, who finally decided to abandon his search for God in the wilderness in order to lead his new bride "back in the fortress of reality," to St. Paul. Safe there from the insecurity of the frontier, this early "God-Seeker" became a successful contractor, and the fictional ancestor of George F. Babbitt. Like his creator, this Lewisian hero early sought God in the "Free Air" of the Western wilderness, and regarded the stodgy business men with a satiric eye. But like his creator, he later went "back in the fortress of reality," and regarded his early idealism as romantic and unreal.

Like many Americans and most realists, Lewis conceived of Reality in two ways. The first Reality included all the facts of life—both the material and the ideal, the ugly and the beautiful, the dull and the romantic. But the second "reality" included only the status quo of existing society—usually materialistic, and ugly, and unromantic. Following the tradition of nineteenth-century "realism," the early Lewis described existing society as materialistic and ugly, in order to urge the reform of the narrow "reality." But the later Lewis increasingly identified this partial "reality" with total Reality, and therefore rejected as unreal that idealism which would reform society and that romance which would escape its existing conventions.

As late as 1935, Lewis could retrospectively describe the years 1885-1935 as "This Golden Half-Century," when "there was romance everywhere, and life, instead of being a dusty routine, was exciting with hope and courage and adventure." For Lewis had been born a romantic and a liberal idealist. "For all his modernity," wrote Vernon Parrington, "Sinclair Lewis is still an echo of Jean Jacques and the golden hopes of the enlightenment." In his youth he had attended the Utopian "Helicon Hall" of Upton Sinclair. And always his heart had sympathized with the rebellious Carol Kennicott, the romantic Babbitt, and the God-seeking scientist, Martin Arrowsmith. The greatness of these earlier novels lay in the romance and idealism which he described as implicit even in the ugly "reality" of Main Street and Zenith.

But progressively as he grew older, Lewis praised those unromantic social realities which he had earlier satirized—although, to be sure, he had always valued them grudgingly. For even in celebrating the youthful freedom of Carol Kennicott, he had valued the unromantic realism of her doctor-husband. And even in sympathizing with the romantic dreams of George F. Babbitt, he had realistically returned him to the fortress of his family at last. Only with his ideal Martin Arrowsmith had he dared to pursue individual freedom to a cabin in the wilderness, and there, like Thoreau, his ideal hero suffered exile from social "reality." But after *Arrowsmith,* Lewis described all his idealistic heroes as either returning abjectly to "the fortress of reality," or miserably failing. So Dodsworth and his wife sought romance in Europe, but found it empty and alien. Ann Vickers sought to reform society, but finally married the realistic judge whom she had earlier sought to indict. And *Work of Art* celebrated a work-a-day hero who abandoned his earlier ideal of creating the perfect hotel in order to make a living for his family in the real world.

All Lewis's novels described the conflict of men's ideals or dreams with the "reality" of things as they are. Some of his earlier novels achieved a measure of greatness by describing these conflicts vividly, and showing why the dreams failed or how the ideals sometimes achieved success. But all the later novels failed by denying the value, or the "reality," of those earlier ideals. By deporting romance to Europe and idealism to Utopia, they made "reality" safe for America. But in so doing, they themselves became unreal.

Disillusionment with the romantic idealism of the nineteenth century has been typical of the realism of the twentieth. But just as the earlier idealism was sometimes confused, so the disillusion has been. For sometimes the earlier idealism was pragmatic, and directed towards the reform or control of "reality": the ideals of the pioneer and the aviator, of the scientist and the doctor, were all realistic. But sometimes the earlier idealism was merely romantic, and directed toward escape from "reality": the dreams of the great lover and the world traveler, of the esthete and the perfectionist, were all unrealistic. When modern realism had described the falsity of the merely romantic ideals of escape, it has been valid. But when it has described all ideals as false, it has become confused and empty.

Lewis's first adult novel described the romantic idealism of *Our Mr. Wrenn,* who dreamed of world travel and free love, and sought them in Europe. But there he met the bohemian Istra Nash, who explained: "When a person is Free, you know, he is never free to be anything but Free." So Mr. Wrenn returned to America, a sadder but wiser man: although his idealism was romantically false, he had learned from it.

Lewis's second adult novel, *The Trail of the Hawk,* described the ideal of the aviator in the modern world. And an early, juvenile novel, *Hike and the Aeroplane,* had also celebrated the romance of flight. But characteristically, *The Hawk* described its hero as an opportunist who failed to realize the pragmatic ideal of man's conquest of the air, and soon lost sight of all his early idealism.

In later years, Lewis compared *The Trail of the Hawk* to the true life-story of Charles Lindbergh, described recently in *The Spirit of St. Louis.* But their differences are more important than their resemblances. The fictional Carl Ericson, the "hawk" of Joralemon, Minnesota, was a farm boy of Scandinavian ancestry like the actual Lindbergh, who, like him, turned mechanic, flew in barnstorming exhibitions, and felt and communicated to others the romance of flight. The first part of *The Trail of the Hawk* vividly prophesies the true story of "the lone eagle." But where Lindbergh focused his energies on his historic conquest of the Atlantic and became an authentic American hero, the fictional Carl Ericson, lacking any focus or heroism, puttered away his life, leaving even aviation at last and ending as a minor promoter. Not only does the second half of *The Trail of the Hawk* fail to realize the promise of its title, but it fails to realize the actual heroism of American reality embodied in "the lone eagle." In long retrospect, the failure of *The Hawk* seems ominous.

The Job is one of the most interesting of Lewis's early novels. The heroine escapes from her Main Street to achieve freedom in the great world, and focuses her energies on her "Job" to achieve success as manager of a chain of hotels. But her name, Una Golden, is probably symbolic: her single-minded concern with the "reality" of business and money largely excludes love, and to her romance is incidental.

Nevertheless she realizes more freedom than the later *Ann Vickers,* and more effective work than the later *Work of Art*—novels which deal more specifically with the freedom of woman, and the dedication of work.

With *Main Street* Lewis achieved fame. And *Main Street* begins with romantic idealism. Dedicated to "James Branch Cabell and Joseph Hergesheimer," its heroine is introduced "on a hill by the Mississippi where Chippewas camped two generations ago," standing with a "quality of suspended freedom." This fictional granddaughter of the pioneer "God-Seeker" of 1850 now questions the "comfortable faith" of Main Street, but after failing to convert her "dull neighbors" or to find romance with her unimaginative husband, she flees to New York and Washington in search of culture and freedom. But this freedom proves empty, and when Will Kennicott comes to woo her back, she returns. "It's so much more complicated than I knew when I put on Ground Grippers and started out to reform the world," she admits. She has failed, and returns to reality: "But I have won in this: I've never excused my failures by sneering at my aspirations." *Main Street* ends with the defeat of romantic idealism, but with the reaffirmation of ideals.

Babbitt achieved greater fame than *Main Street* and was a better novel. It enlarged the scope of the American society which it studied, but its scope does not explain its importance. In *Babbitt,* Lewis almost achieved the realist's ideal of allowing the story to tell itself without apparent interference of author. Where Lewis had obviously sympathized with Carol Kennicott, and later almost identified himself with Martin Arrowsmith, Babbitt is neither hero nor villain, but seems to exist in his own right—the natural product of his society. And through him America seems to reveal itself to the reader.

The archetypal American, George F. Babbitt, accepts the standards of his community without question, and when he revolts from them, does so blindly, as an individual or "natural" man. The natural friend of the sensitive Paul Riesling, he resents the crucifixion of Paul by society. With natural decency, he revolts against the political graft which society seems to take for granted. Seeking freedom from the narrow intolerance of his social group, he dares briefly defend the radical leader of the opposition party. Longing for romance, he indulges in a bohemian love affair. But recognizing that he owes both his past success and his present livelihood to the approval of his society, he finally conforms, returns to "reality," and renounces his former rebellions against the standards of his community.

The change from *Main Street* to *Babbitt* is essentially a change of perspective. In *Main Street*, Lewis and his heroine saw society from the outside—in *Babbitt*, from the inside. The sharpness of the contrast between "ideal" freedom and "reality" therefore has become blunted, and the value of the "aspirations" themselves dubious. Babbitt's friend, Paul Riesling, has shot his wife—is friendship for a criminal good? Babbitt's real estate office has prospered by connivance with graft—who is he to cast the first stone? Radicals are "reds," and therefore un-American—is not friendship with them traitorous? And his "romance" with the bohemian Tanis was obviously an escape from his own dull marriage. Therefore the rebellious and romantic idealism of George F. Babbitt seems not only fore-defeated, but confused. The greatness of the book is that this confusion reveals itself without the apparent intervention of the author. But the weakness of the book is that the author seems to share the confusion.

Just as *Babbitt* described the life of a typical real estate salesman, so Arthur Miller's recent tragic drama describes *The Death of a Salesman*. A comparison of the two is revealing. Both George Babbitt and Willy Loman are confused in their standards—both dream empty dreams, commit adultery, condone dishonesty. But where Babbitt exists in a society where all values are confused, and men succeed chiefly by dishonesty, the confusion of Willy Loman is contrasted with the clear standards of his neighbors, which bring success. The tragic flaw in Babbitt is also that of his society, but the tragic flaw of Loman is that he has mistaken the compromises of his society for its true standards. In *Babbitt*, "reality" seems to deny idealism; but in *Death of a Salesman* reality includes idealism, denying only false dreams. The fault of *Babbitt* is that its author seems to accept the standards (or lack of them) of his hero as the American norm, or, to put it differently, that Lewis equates the very confusion of that American society which he describes, with "Reality."

Arrowsmith, however, seemed to overcome this fault, and to refute this criticism. The "quality of suspended freedom" which Carol Kennicott had failed fully to realize, and which Babbitt had renounced, Martin Arrowsmith now realized to the full. The American idealism which Lewis and his earlier characters had sought constantly in different ways—Lewis himself in Helicon Hall, Mr. Wrenn in European travel, Carl Ericson in the romance of aviation, Una Golden in an independent career, Carol Kennicott in cultural reform, and Babbitt in romantic rebellion—all this idealism Lewis now concentrated in the character of Martin Arrowsmith. Alone among his idealistic heroes, Arrowsmith achieved a measure of success, and even of greatness (Mr. DeVoto to the contrary notwithstanding). And not only did this hero achieve fictional greatness, but he achieved the greatness of fiction—the novel became Lewis's best, not because it described his "best" character, but because it realized him most intensely and completely. *Arrowsmith* seemed to embody and to illustrate the ideal values of its author, and to refute the charges of confusion.

Arrowsmith remains Lewis's best novel and—I think—one of the best American novels. Like *Moby-Dick* and *Huckleberry Finn,* it achieved a balance and a focus which the earlier and the later novels of these American authors lacked. Like *Moby-Dick* it described a heroic quest and, like *Huckleberry Finn,* it spoke the authentic American language. Beyond both, it embodied the modern ideal of the scientist and seeker of truth in a credibly human character. But its minor flaws were also prophetic—like the inflated language of *Moby-Dick,* or the confused conclusion of *Huckleberry Finn.* In minor ways *Arrowsmith* suggested that final divorce of idealism and "reality" which was to confuse Lewis's later novels.

As his letters to his publisher repeat, Lewis intended to entitle *Arrowsmith* "The Barbarian." From his first conception the idealistic character of his hero seemed to him somehow un–American. This pure idealism was inspired by and embodied in the German-born Professor "Gottlieb," whose absolute devotion to truth carried a conviction wholly lacking, for instance, in the later hero of *The God-Seeker.* One of the central conflicts which motivates the story is that between Martin Arrowsmith and the materialistic American society which demands immediate results from his experiments. Probably it is this excessive materialism which prompted Mr. DeVoto's charge that *Arrowsmith* gives a distorted picture of the American Public Health Service and of American research foundations in general. And certainly Arrowsmith is presented as an intransigent individualist, in conflict with American institutions which resemble Boosters Clubs rather than research foundations. The hero's devotion to scientific truth is somewhat too pure, and American society's concern with cash results somewhat too blind.

Nevertheless *Arrowsmith*'s conception of scientific truth is neither "sentimental," nor "trivial." The conflict between the idealism of the scientist and society's demand for immediate results has always been real, and was even more intense when the novel was written. Although the hero is described as an individualist, his conception of truth is in no sense trivial, nor does he ignore the social concept of science—indeed he fails in his attempt to test his "bacteriophage" by means of scientific "control groups," precisely because he is a social being, subject to human weaknesses. When at last he resigns from the "Institute" to devote himself to private research in his cabin-laboratory, he does so without romantic illusions concerning either his own righteousness or his probable success. And on the other hand, his resignation from American "society" repeats that classic pattern of American individualistic idealism, first clearly defined by Thoreau a century earlier.

The minor flaw in the conception of *Arrowsmith,* which was to cause major confusion in the later novels of Sinclair Lewis, is the logical flaw which has lain latent in our American conception of Reality. Social "reality" had often seemed to deny "idealism." Therefore, either the idealist must reject social "reality," or he must abandon his ideals and "return to reality." In *Walden,* Thoreau rejected society, and *Arrowsmith* repeats some of his intransigence. Similarly, the heroes of *Main Street* and *Babbitt* found that society rejected their ideals as romantic, and each to a different degree abandoned his aspirations and "returned to reality." The workable concept of a reality which includes and uses ideals in order to change society has often been ignored by American writers. In his later novels, Lewis conceived of an American "reality" which excluded romance and idealism entirely.

In contrast to *Arrowsmith, Elmer Gantry* described a "hero" who had adopted the opportunist compromises of his society as his ideals. Lacking the scruples of Babbitt, Elmer Gantry took "reality" for his God, and denounced as communistic that idealism which would try to reform society.

On the other hand, *Dodsworth* carried on Babbitt's submerged idealism, and sought in Europe the culture and romance which Babbitt so signally failed to realize in America. But an alien European culture could not fill his life, and for him Europe became a desperate stop-gap. After the break-up of his marriage, he returned to his European love, without hope. And in Lewis's last novel, *World So Wide,* Dodsworth finally reappeared, leading an expatriate existence in Italy, and ironically warning the final hero against the unreality of this rootless European life.

After *Dodsworth,* Lewis won the Nobel Prize, and was hailed as the representative American writer. In his Stockholm address, he bewailed that Americans "have no standards...no heroes to be followed nor villains to be condemned, no certain ways to be pursued and no dangerous paths to be avoided. . . . The American novelist. . . must work alone, in confusion." And three years after returning to America, Lewis published *Ann Vickers* to document this confusion.

All the earlier heroes of Lewis had been idealists of a sort, and he had described their many conflicts with reality in many ways. Sometimes they had succeeded in part, more often they had failed and adjusted to reality, but always he had sympathized with them. Only when *Elmer Gantry* clearly perverted the "yearning" of American romantics did Lewis scorn his hero. Always the author's emotional sympathy with romance and his moral approval of idealism had remained clear. Now *Ann Vickers* embodied an American idealism more complete than any, except *Arrowsmith*. A feminist and social reformer, Ann lived a free life, fought social corruption in all its forms, and sought love in the confusion of a great city. Clearly her author favored her among his heroines. But at the very end, Ann Vickers—to the consternation both of her associates and of her readers—chose to marry an ex-judge who had just been condemned for accepting graft and condoning dishonesty in office. And clearly Sinclair Lewis approved of his heroine's choice of this manly judge, who had scorned the social reformers, but now found himself beaten by them. His idealistic Ann not only renounced her earlier idealism, but fell in love with that "realism" which she had formerly condemned. In *Ann Vickers* Lewis reversed himself and rejected the idealism which had inspired *Arrowsmith:* although the idealistic reformer now triumphed, the tough realist won the heroine's love, and her author's sympathy.

Finally, *Work of Art* reversed the earlier standards of *Main Street* and *Babbitt,* and completed Lewis's confusion. Carol Kennicott had tried vainly to bring art to Gopher Prairie, and Babbitt had embodied that smug philistinism which scorns art. Now *Work of Art* set out to prove fictionally that the art of managing a hotel is just as valid as the art of painting a picture. And the idea was reasonable: if his hero had embodied that quality of imagination which creates new forms—whether of the fine arts or of business management—*Work of Art* might have become a fine novel. But Lewis's hero, although embodying perfectly the ideal of *Work,* not only lacked but positively condemned the ideal of *Art,* or creative idealism. And Lewis's notebooks show that this denial of artistic idealism was conscious and purposeful.

The published novel tells the story of Myron Weagle, the hardworking but unimaginative manager of a series of hotels, and his brother Ora Weagle, the romantic poet who scorns work and continually borrows money from his brother. In the published novel, Myron is the epitome of realism, in its unromantic extreme—honest and plodding, but accepting stolidly the dishonesty of the world and making the best of it. And Ora Weagle is the epitome of romanticism at its worst—dishonest and flamboyant, denouncing the world but living as a parasite upon it. At the end Myron decides, wisely (the author implies), to give up his second-rate hotel and start a motel, because that is the way the business is going. He has never created a truly fine hotel, or "work of art," but he has worked hard and gotten along, and adjusted to reality.

But Lewis's notebooks for *Work of Art* show that he originally conceived of his hero as an idealist who constantly planned to create the perfect hotel. Myron Weagle was to have been an artist, who, unlike his romantic brother Ora, wished to create something real. But (Lewis asked himself in his notebook), is not the "artist" who plans to create an impossibly perfect hotel, just as unrealistic as the poet who writes about impossible beauty and romance? Therefore, Lewis consciously converted his hero from an imaginative artist in hotel-making to a realistic worker in hotel-keeping. Rejecting *Art*, Sinclair Lewis idealized *Work*. And in so doing he destroyed not only the significance of this novel, with its challenging title, but of his later novels which followed this pattern. The representative American artist, renouncing vision, retreated into the fortress of reality, and (artistically speaking) perished.

The decline and fall of Sinclair Lewis—typical American novelist —illustrates an American tragedy. The idealist, recognizing that his vision of perfection is impossible, renounces his vision and "returns to reality." Or, clinging to his ideals in spite of their certain defeat, he may become a fanatic—as in *Kingsblood Royal;* or a rootless expatriate— as in *Dodsworth* and *World So Wide.* The realist, on the other hand, denounces all idealism as romantic, because unrealizable, or because it threatens the "reality" of things as they are. In whatever form, this American tragedy of "all or nothing" exiles the idealist from reality and even declares him to be "un-American."

But the earlier novels of Sinclair Lewis—especially those which made him spokesman for his generation—described the conflict of American idealism and materialism in pragmatic or in comic terms. Though the cultural enthusiasm of Carol Kennicott was sometimes comically exaggerated, it embodied an impulse not only ideal, but pragmatically possible, so that the Main Streets of today hear more of the music and read more of the books that Carol urged. And though the scientific idealism of Arrowsmith was sometimes narrowly individualistic, his celebration of "pure science" influenced the practice even of modern industrial research, and his realization of the heroism of the "microbe hunters," even though partial, gave modern American fiction one of its few authentic heroes.

Lewis lived through "the golden half-century" of America, and realized some of its glory. But when he renounced the glory, and retreated in confusion to the fortress of reality, both he and his America became the poorer.

Martin Arrowsmith: The Scientist as Hero

Charles E. Rosenberg

With the manuscript of *Babbitt* almost complete in the fall of 1921, Sinclair Lewis already planned his next novel. "Perhaps," he wrote Alfred Harcourt, his friend and publisher, it would not be satiric at all, "rebellious as ever,... but the central character *heroic.*" His next novel was *Arrowsmith*. Its heroic protagonist is a research scientist, the first of consequence in American fiction. To Sinclair Lewis he was far more than that.

Martin Arrowsmith is a new kind of hero, one appropriate to twentieth-century America. Journalists and historians tirelessly inform us that the 1920s were years of intense and aggressive materialism. Yet Arrowsmith is quite obviously a hero not of deeds, but of the spirit. His scientific calling is not a concession to material values, but a means of overcoming them. In the austere world of pure science and in the example of Max Gottlieb, Arrowsmith finds a system of values which guide and sanction his stumbling quest for personal integrity. It is this quest which provides the novel's moral structure. Martin Arrowsmith's professional career is the record of his deepening understanding and acceptance of these scientific values and of their role in assuring Arrowsmith's ultimate triumph in his struggles with a succession of increasingly plausible material temptations.

Other centuries have accepted patterns into which such moral

From *American Quarterly* 15, no. 3 (Fall 1963). © 1963 by the American Studies Association.

achievement could be projected—the martyr, the pilgrim, the evangelist and, in more recent generations, the creative artist. None of these seemed particularly relevant to Sinclair Lewis in 1922. He had emphatically rejected the forms of traditional religion, despite the appeal which they had held for him as a lonely adolescent. Religion had become just another marketable commodity; its purveyors could not easily be pictured as heroic. Nor was the sensitive artist a potential hero; Lewis knew too many and knew them too well. Yet Sinclair Lewis was very much a novelist of society, very much bound to the particular. His hero had to have a vocation. The problem was to find one in which dignity and integrity could be maintained in a world of small compromise and petty accommodation.

Yet America did have a heritage of dignity and individualism, Lewis believed. It lay in the pioneering spirit of the men and women who had settled the nation's West. Their heroic qualities had created America, yet theirs were the very characteristics which seemed to be disappearing most rapidly in a twentieth-century America, settled and implacably confining. *Arrowsmith* begins with an almost crudely pointed vignette: Martin Arrowsmith's great-grandmother, aged fourteen, is seated at the reins of a wagon. Her father, lying racked with fever in the wagon's bed, begs her to turn aside and ask shelter at her uncle's. But she will be obligated to no one and turns the wagon west. "They's a whole lot of new things I aim to be seeing," she exclaims. On the opening page of *Main Street,* Lewis describes another restless young girl. Carol Milford, like Arrowsmith, is the descendent of pioneers. Though the days of their exploits are "deader than Camelot," the spirit of her daring ancestors survives to animate this rebellious girl. In the future Mrs. Kennicott, however, the divine discontent which helped people a continent becomes an unfocused and almost pathetic dissatisfaction with the commonplace world of Gopher Prairie. Arrowsmith is gifted with the same vigor and curiosity—but is able to attain through it the heroic stature denied Carol. In the life of the pure scientist he discovers a vocation in which his spiritual endowments find meaningful and constructive expression.

During the early part of 1922, the *Century Magazine* published a series of anonymous articles attacking the pretensions of American medicine. The articles were entitled "Our Medicine Men," and written by Paul de Kruif, a junior staff member at the Rockefeller Institute. By the end of 1922 he was unemployed.

In the summer of 1922, Sinclair Lewis still sought a suitable protagonist for his heroic novel. He had begun his customarily detailed
research for a novel of the American labor movement, its hero to be a
Christlike leader modeled after Eugene Debs. But the novel did not
seem to coalesce. On a hot August day in Chicago, Morris Fishbein,
associate editor of the *Journal of the American Medical Association,* introduced Lewis to the young bacteriologist from the Rockefeller Institute. *Arrowsmith* was the result of this meeting. No one but Sinclair
Lewis could have written quite such a novel, yet insofar as *Arrowsmith*
is a comment on the world of American medicine and biological research,
insofar as it makes use of scientific values and preoccupations, it re-
flects clearly the attitudes of Paul de Kruif.

De Kruif provided Lewis with the *vitae* for his principal characters, with the details of laboratory procedure and with a plausible
scientific setting for Arrowsmith's exploits. Even more important,
Lewis believed, was his contribution of the scientist's "philosophy."
De Kruif entertained few doubts concerning the nature of the scientific
endeavor or of the intellectual and personal integrity it demanded. He
was equally certain that most American research was slipshod and
careless, simply cluttering the journals and indices. De Kruif's influence can be documented not only in Sinclair Lewis's own words, but
in the youthful bacteriologist's published writings. Before the appearance of *Arrowsmith* in March of 1925, he had written, in addition to the
articles in the *Century,* an essay on Jacques Loeb which appeared in
Harper's and the section on medicine, also anonymous, in Harold
Stearn's *Civilization in the United States.* His discussion of Loeb, both in
Harper's and in Sterns's *Civilization,* is particularly significant, for it
is Jacques Loeb's values which are those professed by Max Gottlieb.
De Kruif's "philosophy" is not a philosophy at all, but the recent
convert's overenthusiastic reflection of a philosophy—of Loeb's biological mechanism.

Loeb's methodological scruples, even his style of life, had, moreover, a particular significance for American medicine in the early
1920s. He lived and expressed the gospel of pure science. In at least a
limited sense, *Arrowsmith* is an incident in the birth of a new scientific
medicine. De Kruif's hostility toward the medical profession is an
extreme, though not unrepresentative, instance of the laboratory scientist's hostility toward the clinician. Such attitudes, formed in the
uneasy coexistence between laboratory and clinical medicine, shaped

many of the particular incidents and emphases in *Arrowsmith*.

Martin Arrowsmith's professional biography is a record not only of the progress of a confused and easily misled young man toward emotional and intellectual fulfillment; it is the recapitulation in one man's life of the development of medicine in the United States. Each stage of Arrowsmith's career corresponds to a particular stage in the evolution of American medicine. Doc Vickerson's practice—and Martin's own practice in Wheatsylvania—dramatizes, for example, the trails and rewards of what de Kruif called "the splendid old type of general practitioner." Both he and Lewis were sympathetic to this aspect of American medicine. It seemed informal, individual, at moments even heroic; at least it was free of that mixture of ersatz science and sordid commercialism which de Kruif regarded as having corrupted contemporary medical practice.

At Winnemac University, both teachers and classmates of young Arrowsmith exemplify particular types and trends in medicine's coming-of-age. Dean Silva, for example, the pious disciple of Osler and Laënnec, represents the understanding and craftsmanship to be found in clinical medicine. Professor Robertshaw, the self-exiled Brahmin physiologist, who always spoke—with elaborate casualness —of his student days in Leipzig with Carl Ludwig, illustrates the transference of German laboratory medicine to the United States— and with his "fussy little. . .maiden-aunt experiments" proves that the progress of science demands the spirit and not simply the techniques of German science. Roscoe Geake, the professor of otolaryngology and future minion of the New Idea Instrument and Furniture Company, is a representative of the most sordid and ignoble aspects of clinical medicine, his specialism simply a device for the multiplication of fees.

Unlike most of his fellow medical students, Arrowsmith is the graduate of a four-year liberal arts curriculum. He is confident in his abilities as he enters medical school and looks forward to increasing his scientific knowledge. But, except for the inspiring example of Max Gottlieb, he is to be sadly disappointed. Arrowsmith's disillusionment is identical with that experienced by a hypothetical college graduate whose medical career was depicted by Paul de Kruif in the *Century*. He

> enters his first medical course with confidence, aware of his
> superiority over the majority of his fellows. It is easy, then,

to imagine his dismay when he discovers that he knows far more of physics and chemistry than many of his medical instructors, and finds himself surrounded by glib-memoried, poorly-prepared ignoramuses who shine by reason of their parrot-like ability to reel off an enormous number of facts crammed out of text-books.

After a short residency at a metropolitan hospital, an experience which at first stimulates then bores him, Arrowsmith begins practice in Wheatsylvania, North Dakota. But a newly inspired enthusiasm for public-health work earns him only the scorn of the small farming community. Fortunately, he is able to leave. Through the agency of Max Gottlieb and Gustaf Sondelius, he obtains a position with the health department of a small Iowa city. In Nautilus, Arrowsmith's zeal quickly fades before the boosterism of his chief, the improbable Almus Pickerbaugh. Public-health programs, Martin discovers, are to be prosecuted in newspaper columns and on the lecture platform, not in the laboratory. De Kruif had, before meeting Lewis, recorded his intense dislike for such "shouters for public health," for these "dubious Messiahs who combine the zealous fanaticism of the missionary with the Jesuitical cynicism of the politician." Boards of health, he argued, should be administered by engineers, statisticians and bacteriologists—not by half-educated physicians.

Driven finally from his post in Nautilus, Arrowsmith is forced to accept a position with that "most competent, most clean and brisk and visionless medical factory, the Rouncefield Clinic." In the early years of the 1920s, the clinic seemed to all observers the most advanced form of medical practice. And de Kruif, like many other laboratory men, had already demonstrated his distaste for these gilded repair shops. Research, Arrowsmith soon learns, is regarded simply as a means of securing free advertising for the clinic. After a year of bondage at the Rouncefield Clinic, Arrowsmith's first paper is published in the *Journal of Infectious Diseases* and he is offered a research position at the McGurk Institute (of course, Lewis's conception of the Rockefeller Institute). At first Arrowsmith feels that he has reached a kind of scientific Elysium. He has a well-equipped laboratory, competent assistants, the company of his revered Max Gottlieb. Yet this too proves less than idyllic. Its demand for social graces, for premature publication, in short, its cultivation of success leads Arrowsmith toward his final and most important decision. He resigns from the Institute and joins his friend, the irreverent chemist Terry Wickett, who had already fled the compromising security of McGurk, at a wooded Vermont lake. Here, with a few like-minded investigators, they plan to conduct years of uninterrupted research. Thus the novel ends; Arrowsmith has conquered the final and most plausible obstacle in his quest for personal integrity—he has renounced success itself. Or at least success by the ordinary standards of American life. Like Max Gottlieb Martin Arrowsmith is destined for fame, but in a world whose judgments are eternal, international and ultimately untouched by material considerations.

One of the tentative titles for *Arrowsmith* was *The Shadow of Max Gottlieb*. An unfortunate title perhaps, but in a way justified. For Gottlieb *is* the scientific vocation. He had, inevitably, to be German. It is not simply that Paul de Kruif was immensely impressed by Jacques Loeb. To the young men of Lewis's and de Kruif's generation, science was German science, its embodiment the German professor. Gottlieb is a symbol not only of the transfer of European knowledge and techniques to the New World, but an expression of the peculiar mystique of German academic life. His worship of research *qua* research and his reverent attitude toward this pursuit of knowledge are very much the product of the German university. Such beliefs never established themselves with quite such intensity in France, in England—or in the United States. Yet the almost religious texture of this attitude toward the scientist's task is essential to the moral structure of the novel. It clothes Arrowsmith's long hours in his laboratory with a spiritual, an inherently transcendent quality.

As in the legends of the saints, every sordid aspect of Max Gottlieb's life is only evidence of his grace and a comment upon the tawdry standards of those who mock him. He lives in a "small brown weedy" house, rides to his laboratory on an ancient and squeaky bicycle, and wears the shabby topcoat of a poor professor. Most Americans could only regard him as something of a crank. His was "no work for the tall man at a time when heroes were building bridges, experimenting with Horseless Carriages, writing the first of the poetic Compelling Ads, and selling miles of calico and cigars." Yet on the crowded desk in Gottlieb's little bungalow, letters from the "great ones" of Europe awaited his reply—and mocked the collective wisdom of Mohalis and Wheatsylvania and Sauk Centre. But Arrowsmith is vouchsafed the grace to understand and find inspiration in

Max Gottlieb's life and ideas. Arrowsmith too shares something of his curiosity, something of his indignation at the shoddy and imprecise.

Sinclair Lewis created Max Gottlieb, but with raw materials provided by Paul de Kruif. Gottlieb, de Kruif later recalled, was an amalgam of Frederick G. Novy and Jacques Loeb. Novy was the austere and scientifically elegant professor of bacteriology at the University of Michigan who introduced de Kruif to biological research. Loeb was his idol at the Rockefeller Institute. Though Gottlieb is a bacteriologist and immunologist like Novy, not a general physiologist like Loeb, his personality and mannerisms obviously represent the novelist's rendering of the articulate and sardonic German—or at least the picture of him which de Kruif had presented to Lewis. In his recently published memoir, Paul de Kruif describes Gottlieb as a "muddy mélange" of Novy and Loeb. There is little evidence, however, of his having been dissatisfied with this sentimentally didactic figure when, in 1924, he first read the manuscript of *Arrowsmith.*

The genuine scientists in *Arrowsmith,* Gottlieb, Terry Wickett and Arrowsmith himself, all share the same conception of truth. It is knowledge obtained in rigidly controlled experiments, knowledge analyzed and expressed in quantitative terms. There is only one assurance in life, Gottlieb warns the youthful Arrowsmith: "In this vale of tears there is nothing certain but the quantitative method." Though many biologists today would approve such methodological sentiments, they would hardly express them with such passionate conviction. Our contemporaries are almost a century removed from the philosophical preoccupations which meant so much in Jacques Loeb's youth. The emotional intensity with which he, and his fictional counterpart Max Gottlieb, express such quantitative goals is clearly the reflection of an ancient conflict within the scientific community. This is the struggle between vitalism and mechanism.

Physical chemistry and mathematics were more than a method to Jacques Loeb; they were his reason for becoming a biologist. He had, he recalled, read Schopenhauer and Eduard von Hartmann as a very young man. And while a student of philosophy at Berlin, the problem of free will seemed to him the most central of intellectual concerns. Loeb soon found himself unable to accept the existence of such individual freedom. Nor could he accept the techniques of philosophical analysis traditionally employed in the discussion of such problems. Loeb turned to physiological research in an attempt to prove that animal behavior was simply the sum of inorganic phenomena no different in kind from those studied by the physical scientist. Human behavior too, he believed, was no more nor less than the product of such physical and chemical forces. The "mystical" aspects of life were to be dissolved in the acid of mathematics and physical chemistry.

Naturphilosophie had been thoroughly vanquished by the late 1840s; yet the struggle against it had left a lasting impression on German biological thought. The men most articulate in opposing formal idealism were imbued with an instinctive sensitivity to philosophical implications and many embraced mechanistic materialism with an absolutist zeal inevitably paralleling the idealistic convictions of an earlier generation. It was this period of conflicting ideologies which shaped Loeb's intense and consistently generalizing mind.

Jacques Loeb was, for example, an assistant of Adolf Fick. Fick was one of the greatest of Carl Ludwig's students and perhaps the one most inclined toward the study of physiological processes in physical and mathematical terms. And Ludwig—with his great colleagues Helmholtz, du Bois-Reymond and Bürck—had been a leader in the struggle against a romantic or purely descriptive biology. Loeb himself always regarded the significance of his classic experiments on artificial parthenogenesis "to be the fact that they transfer the problem of fertilization from the realm of morphology into the realm of physical chemistry." His earlier investigations of animal tropisms were, he explained, crucial because they proved that animal movements were regulated "by the law of mass action." (Max Gottlieb remarks to Arrowsmith when the young man arrives at McGurk, that he hopes "to bring immunity reactions under the mass action law.") When Gottlieb feels that Arrowsmith has learned the elementary principles of his trade, he warns that true scientific competence requires a knowledge of higher mathematics and physical chemistry. "All living things are physio-chemical," he points out to his disciple; "how can you expect to make progress if you do not know physical chemistry, and how can you know physical chemistry without much mathematics?" Arrowsmith's maturity as a scientist comes only in the last few pages of the book. His papers are praised in Paris and Brussels and Cambridge. But the socially impeccable Dr. Holabird is simply bewildered. "What," he asks, did Arrowsmith "think he was anyway—a bacteriologist or a biophysicist?"

In a very real sense, the values which sanction and direct Arrow-

smith's quest for truth reflect those of Jacques Loeb and of a genera-
tions-old debate within the academic confines of German biology. As
I have suggested, moreover, Max Gottlieb's values record accurately
the laboratory scientist's impatience with the impressionistic and
empirical aspects of clinical medicine. The physician could not, in the
nature of things, be truly a scientist. The essence of medicine is the
functional relationship which the individual physician bears to his
patient. It is his task to heal—or at least to console. It is the scientist's
task to understand. At best, de Kruif argued in 1922, the physician is a
skilled technician of applied science. The attempt to train each practitioner as a scientist was simply delusive; a return to the preceptorial
system of medical education would be preferable. Lewis too found it
natural to accept the pure scientist's vocation as a higher one. The very
social necessity which created the medical profession tied it to the
exigencies of everyday life, to compromise and commercialism, to the
collection of bills and the lancing of boils. As able, self-sacrificing and
understanding as the best physician might be, he could never transcend the social relationships which formed the fabric of his professional existence. And to Lewis the essence of heroism, the gauge of a
man's stature, lay in the extent to which he was able to disengage
himself from the confining pressures of American society. His heroic
protagonist had to be a scientist; he could not be a physician. And
certainly not an American physician.

Both de Kruif and Lewis agreed that American society had de-
based even the pursuit of science. For both men the essential factor in
scientific progress was the initiative and creativity of the individual
investigator. There seemed increasingly little provision for such individualism in twentieth-century America. To de Kruif, no development within American science was more dangerous than its growing
"barrack spirit." Centralization and bureaucratization of scientific
research were not simply the inevitable concomitants of an increasing
complexity within society and within the body of scientific knowledge—they were developments inimical to the impulse of spontaneous
creativity. Hence Lewis's acid portraits of Rippleton Holabird, of
A. De Witt Tubbs and of his League of Cultural Agencies. ("If men like
Koch and Pasteur only had such a system," Tubbs bubbles to Martin,
"how much more *scope* their work might have had! Efficient universal
cooperation—that's the thing in science today—the time of this silly
jealous, fumbling individual research has gone by.") The young scien-

tist, in an unfortunate image of de Kruif's, was to be denied the "privi-lege of wandering forth equipped only with the rifle of his intelligence, and thus to remain for long periods of lawless and impudent penetra-tion of the forests and jungles of ignorance." No greater man had ever drawn his inspiration from the memo pad of a research coordinator. Their hypotheses, de Kruif argued, were drawn directly from the observation of natural phenomena. The investigator who sought his inspiration in a library could hardly be considered a scientist at all.

Jacques Loeb was fond of aphorisms. He was especially fond of one coined by his friend and teacher, that great botanist Julius von Sachs. "All originality," Sachs observed, "comes from reading." Loeb was acutely conscious of history and of the communal nature of the scientific endeavor. He might mock the institutions of science and the mediocrities who so often found shelter within such institutional bul-warks, but he realized the futility of rejecting the scientific community as such. He died full of honors on the staff of the Rockefeller Institute. J. H. Northrop, model for Terry Wickett, even though a lover of the outdoors, always maintained his academic connections. Neither Loeb nor Northrop was a failure; neither renounced the corruptions of aca-demic science and both learned to live with success. Even the criticisms and preoccupations of the restless Paul de Kruif were, as I hope to have shown, themselves characteristic products of the intellectual and insti-tutional history of the biological and medical sciences. The conclusion of *Arrowsmith* is not only an indictment of the handicaps placed in the scientist's path by American society, it is a rejection at the same time of the scientific community whose values justify this indictment.

The novels of Sinclair Lewis are peopled with the wistful figures of Americans whose spiritual potentialities are unfulfilled. Arrow-smith is a conspicuous exception. Paul Riesling in *Babbitt* and Frank Shallard in *Elmer Gantry,* for example, were gifted with something of the sensitivity granted Arrowsmith. But unlike him, neither was able to enter a vocation in which his spiritual endowments could find expression. Their inability to conform brought only their own destruction. The tragedy of George Babbitt lies in the pathetic and overwhelming de-feat administered his vague idealism by the forces of organized Zenith. In the scientist's life, however, such chronic questionings find a recog-nized social function. Even Arrowsmith's social inadequacies, his lack of humor, his callousness toward the old and the lonely and the work-ingman are simply evidences of his spiritual stature. It is the small people who make good administrators, who are attuned enough to the petty circumstances of life to function successfully within them.

It is this pervading air of compromise which finally drives Arrowsmith from his wife, from his child and from his laboratory in New York. His ultimate rejection of society and its demands has been criticized as callow romanticism—and perhaps it is. But it is the logical result of Lewis's desire to depict greatness and his inability to conceive of its being allowed to exist within American society.

The Paper-Doll Characters of Sinclair Lewis's *Arrowsmith*

Marilyn Morgan Helleberg

By skillful manipulation of the paper-doll characters in *Arrowsmith*, Sinclair Lewis attacks a society which interferes with scientific individualism. Critic Robert Cantwell, in his essay "Sinclair Lewis," summarizes the belabored point of the novel: "The message of *Arrowsmith*, however Lewis might deny that it was his intention to preach it, was simply that American society was death to any disinterested scientific effort" (*Sinclair Lewis: A Collection of Critical Essays,* ed. Mark Schorer). It cannot be denied that the message leaps out at the reader from almost every page in the novel. It is impossible to ignore Lewis's contention, but it is also difficult to accept the validity of a thesis which is demonstrated by the actions of contrived, stereotyped characters.

The *Arrowsmith* paper dolls are either black or white, and the two groups are separated by a too-neatly drawn line. On the white side are the lonely, suffering rebels, the truth-seekers, the idealists who are true to their own inner nobility, and the complementary characters. Max Gottlieb, the eccentric European laboratory scientist, devoted to scientific individualism, is not an individual but a representative of a type. Alfred Kazin, in *On Native Grounds: An Interpretation of Modern American Prose Literature,* notes of Gottlieb:

> [He] was not merely a European scientist; he was *the* European scientist, the very incarnation of the indescribable cultivation and fathomless European wisdom—a man on

From *The Mark Twain Journal* 14, no. 2 (Summer 1968). © 1968 by Thomas Penney.

speaking terms with Leonardo, Brahms, and Nietzsche; a scientist whose classic work on immunology only seven men in all the world could understand; a cosmopolitan who could prepare exotic little sandwiches for his grubby co-workers.

Lewis's description of Martin Arrowsmith's first encounter with Gottlieb clearly reveals a stereotype:

> On the stone steps of the Main Medical, appeared beneath the arc-light a tall figure, ascetic, self-contained, apart. He did not hurry, like the belated home-bodies. He was unconscious of the world. He looked at Martin and through him; he moved away, muttering to himself, his shoulders stooped, his long hands clasped behind him. He was lost in the shadows, himself a shadow.
>
> He had worn the threadbare top-coat of a poor professor yet Martin remembered him as wrapped in a black velvet cape with a silver star arrogant on his breast.

Gustaf Sondelius, also on the white side of the line, was the soldier of science. "He held reasonable and lengthy degrees, but he was a rich man and eccentric. He roamed the world fighting epidemics and founding institutions and making inconvenient speeches and trying new drinks." To Martin, Sondelius was not a man but a symbol of the war on disease.

Aggressive, slangy, dedicated Terry Wickett also stands clearly on the side of the rebels, giving up everything for his work:

> Martin perceived that Wickett's snarls were partly a resentment, as great as Gottlieb's, of the morphological scientists who ticket things with the nicest little tickets, who name things and rename them and never analyze them. Wickett often worked all night; he was to be seen in shirt-sleeves, his sulky red hair rumpled, sitting with a stop-watch before a temperature bath for hours.

Though Wickett's character is a bit more plausible than that of Gottlieb or Sondelius, he, too, is typecast. Cut out of paper to Lewis's specifications, his actions and reactions are confined within the narrow limits of the author's single-dimensional view of the dedicated scientist.

Martin Arrowsmith is Mr. Truth-seeker. T. K. Whipple, one of Lewis's severest critics, describes Martin's struggle:

> In *Arrowsmith*, Lewis has devoted all of a long book to the tribulations of a seeker for truth in the United States. Before he finally takes refuge in the wilds of Vermont where he can pursue his researches undisturbed, he encounters all the difficulties which the United States puts in the way of a doctor and an investigator who would like to be honest. He is offered every possible inducement to prostitute himself to an easy success . . . but he is unable to cope with an ineluctable honesty and stubborn drive in himself. In the end, he succumbs to his own integrity.
>
> ("Sinclair Lewis," ed. Schorer)

Even Arrowsmith is not three-dimensional. He is a man with a dominant trait (his drive toward scientific individualism), which has the appearance of being assumed for effect. Though he sometimes appears to pass back and forth over the dividing line between black and white, his feet never really touch ground. Columnist Walter Lippmann comments that "Arrowsmith is saved by embracing the religion of science . . . but the religion which [he] embraces, ascetic, disinterested, purified, is for Lewis like some fine mystery seen at a distance" ("Sinclair Lewis," ed. Schorer). Hans Zinsser, in *Rats, Lice, and History,* declares that "if an epidemiologist on a plague study talked and behaved in the manner of the hero of *Arrowsmith,* he would not only be useless, but he would be regarded as something of a yellow ass and a nuisance by his associates." Lewis is not interested in Martin as an individual. He uses him as bait for luring the black paper dolls into his social display case. Martin is Lewis's means of exposing the commercialism of medical schools, the quackery of general practitioners, the politics and fraud of Public Health Departments, the more refined commercialism of metropolitan clinics, the social and financial temptations inherent in institutes for research, and the false values of a middle-class society. Though Martin passes through innumerable temptations and pressures, the emphasis is not on his inner struggle, but upon forces outside himself. The focus is upon the parade of *forces* acting upon him and his reactions to each merely serve to keep the plot going so that Lewis may proceed to his exemplification of the *next* negative and external force against his hero. Alfred Kazin notes:

> With his lonely suffering rebels, he [Lewis] attains not an
> average type but an average myth; and though Lewis ad-
> mires them and suffers with them, the characters he gives
> them are just those which the artist-rebels, the men who are
> "different" would seem to possess by average standards.

In addition to the rebels, there are three complementary characters in the novel who earn their positions on the white side of the line
not because of what they are or what they do, but because of what they
are not and what they refrain from doing. Martin's first wife, Leora,
his friend Clif Clawson, and the object of his infatuation, Orchid Pickerbaugh, are acceptable to Martin and to Lewis because they do not
interfere with Arrowsmith's dedication to science. Leora is considered
by most reviewers to be Lewis's most successful characterization, but
even she lacks depth. T. K. Whipple has this to say about her:

> Leora, Martin's first wife, is by general consent Lewis's
> masterpiece in the creation of character. Not only is she
> likeable, but she is indubitably real . . . yet even Leora inter-
> ests Lewis less than his national portrait gallery of typical
> frauds and fakirs. He prefers to stay safely on the surface of
> social appearances. He shows little of Sherwood Anderson's
> hunger to delve into the lives of men and women.

Leora is too perfect. She is the ideal marital companion for the aspiring
scientific researcher who encourages him, at every turn, to remain
faithful to his ideal. Her only discernable fault is her carelessness about
her appearance, which is a purely external thing. As with all of his
characters, Lewis touches only the surface of Leora, and she merges
more as a wish than as a reality. Dorothy Thompson wrote in her
diary: "Leora, more than any character whom I can remember in fiction, represents the sexual ideal of the truly dynamic and creative
male." What flesh-and-blood wife would say to her husband at the
close of his affair with another woman: "Sandy, dear, I know how you
feel about losing your Orchid. It's sort of Youth going. She really is a
peach. Honestly, I can appreciate how you feel, and sympathize with
you . . ."? Sherwood Anderson's observation about Lewis's characterizations could be applied to Leora:

> There can be no doubt that this man, with his sharp journal-
> istic nose for news of the outer surface of our lives, has
> found out a lot about us and the way we live in our towns

and cities but I am very sure that in the life of every man, woman and child in the country there are forces at work that seem to have escaped the notice of Mr. Lewis. . . . Reading Mr. Sinclair Lewis, one comes inevitably to the conclusion that here is a man writing who, wanting passionately to love the life about him, cannot bring himself to do so, and who, wanting perhaps to see beauty descend upon our lives like a rainstorm, has become blind to the minor beauties our lives hold.

("Sinclair Lewis," ed. Schorer)

Lewis would *like* to find a woman like Leora, but he would be unable to accept any flaws in her personality, so he creates a dream to serve as Martin's helpmate.

The other two complementary characters are "white" in a negative sense. Orchid is harmless because she is a nonentity. Clif Clawson is the typical hale and hardy, well-met extrovert. He is not a rebel, but he is treated sympathetically because he is neither a pretender nor an improver.

The paper dolls on the black side of the line so far outnumber their opponents that it becomes obvious that they are the real subjects of the novel. Of these, Dr. Almus Pickerbaugh, the jingle-writing, hypocritical public health officer and politician, is the most ridiculous. Lewis treats him with satirical humor, whereas the other blacks are the objects of Lewis's abusive invective. Typical of Pickerbaugh's poetic devices is the following:

> Zenith welcomes with high hurraw
> A friend in Almus Pickerbaugh,
> The two-fisted fightin' poet doc
> Who stands for health like Gibraltar's rock.
> He's jammed with figgers and facts and fun,
> The plucky old, lucky ol' son-of-a-gun!

The reader is allowed to laugh at Pickerbaugh while condemning him, and this attitude is a relief. If his characterization were not so obviously contrived for a purpose, it would be easier to accept Lewis's judgment of him.

Ira Hinkley typifies Lewis's disdain for evangelical Christians. He is a medical Elmer Gantry, though less malicious. When Fatty Pfaff remarks that Hinkley is at least sincere, Martin replies, "Sincere? Hell! So is a cockroach!" Though Hinkley appears and reappears throughout the novel, the only trait he ever displays is his assumed piety. He is clearly a representation of a type. Other medical stereotypes include Robertshaw, the pompous, ineffective professor of physiology; Angus Duer, the studious four-flusher; Dr. Roscoe Geake, the commercialistic otolaryngologist who "believed that tonsils had been placed in the human organism for the purpose of providing specialists with closed motors"; Dr. Tubbs and Rippleton Holabird, the commercialists of the drug industry; and the general practitioners of Wheatsylvania, who are, naturally, quacks. "To parade such heresies in the face of the progressive American public is," according to Vernon Louis Parrington, "enough to damn any man, genius or not." Robert Morss Lovett, writing of Lewis as "An Interpreter of American Life," observes that "Mr. Lewis is determined to leave no stone of the medical edifice unturned, and under each he finds human nature in reptilian form" (ed. Schorer). Are we to assume, then, that only the disinterested medical researcher who finds fulfillment in escape is of value to society? Are all general practitioners quacks and all public health officials fraudulent? This is the inevitable conclusion to be drawn if we accept Lewis's portrayal of them. These stereotypes are never counterbalanced by men of integrity in the same positions. Devoted, disinterested researchers are indispensible to the medical profession, but must all others be condemned in order to make the point?

It may be argued that Lewis is a satirist and must employ such half-truths in order to emphasize his contentions, but is he really a satirist? Thrall, Hibbard, and Holman, in *A Handbook to Literature*, define satire in these words:

> A literary manner which blends a critical attitude with humor and wit *to the end that human institutions or humanity may be improved.* The true satirist is conscious of the frailty of institutions of man's devising and attempts through laughter *not so much to tear them down as to inspire a remodeling* (italics not in the original).

With the exception of the characterization of Pickerbaugh, Lewis employs very little humor in his condemnation. As S. P. B. Mais sees it, in *Some Modern Authors,* "Lewis expends all his energy in purely destructive criticism." Certainly, he admits no hope of "remodeling." It is all quite hopeless, and Lewis puts these thoughts in Martin's mind: "God help any man that likes his work and his wife! He's beaten from the beginning." His rebel heroes either succumb to the pressures or escape into a never-never-land where they can shut out the world. In an article published in *American Literature,* Dening Brown says, "Arrowsmith's resolution of his rebellion is one of escape, since he takes refuge in a hermit-like existence as a pure scientist." As Maxwell Geismar states it in "The Land of Faery" (ed. Schorer):

> So all this eloquence and artistic vitality operates in a vacuum in the end. You could say that the whole import of Lewis's work shows that he has learned nothing, answered nothing, solved nothing.

In "Our Photography: Sinclair Lewis" (ed. Schorer), E. M. Forster claims:

> One can safely class him with writers termed advanced, with people who prefer truth to comfort, passion to stability, prevention to cure. But the classification lets what is most vital in him escape; his attitude, though it exists, does not dwell in the depth of his being.

Whipple summarizes the result of Lewis's fatal limitations as a satirist by stating that "the net result of Lewis's work is not a truer apprehension or a deeper insight, but an increase in mutual dissatisfaction." This fact is made all the more tragic because of what Lewis might have been had he been less conscious of his own battle scars. "The satirist, like the jailer, is the victim of his own system of punishment," says Lewis Mumford in "The America of Sinclair Lewis" (ed. Schorer). Mumford believes:

> Were he not driven by some inner exacerbation to "get back at" the community that produced him, Mr. Lewis could give back much to it; for he has real insight and might easily create characters on a large scale who would exist in their own right, not merely as creatures in a malicious demonstration.

It is interesting to note that Sinclair Lewis denied that he was a satirist and claimed to be a romantic; so even if half-truths *were* acceptable in satire, he could not claim justification for his flat paper-doll characters under that label.

The critics agree that Lewis's weak characterizations greatly reduce the literary merit of his novels, but many of them side with Mark Schorer, who insists that "the power of the creation lies in these very limitations. This deficiency contributes to the force of his image, for it permits his characters no escape." Kazin admits that "Lewis's characters have often been criticized as 'types' and they are, partly because he memorialized some of them as such," but he defends Lewis's approach:

> What is really significant in his use of types is that his mind moved creatively in their channels. Lewis has been able to invest his stereotypes with a careless energy that other writers would not have been able to understand much less share, since they did not work so close to the surface.

Schorer was able to perceive something valuable in Lewis's intentionally limited view of his characters:

> Lewis had a particularly narrow and feeble perspective, but given the character of his achievement, its force paradoxically rests upon its narrowness. For its narrowness projects a very sharply defined image.

What is the value of a sharply defined image if that image is only a half-truth? Max Gottlieb has this to say about half-truths: "The scientist is intensely religious—he is so religious that he will not accept half-truths, because they are an insult to his faith." Would Lewis, then, condemn his own writing? Lippman asserts, "Mr. Lewis has an extraordinary talent for inventing stereotypes. A man with a greater instinct for reality would have remembered that life is not so simple. But what he would have gained in truthfulness, he would have lost in influence."

Are paper dolls, then, more effective influences for good than human beings?

Arrowsmith: Genesis, Development, Versions

Lyon N. Richardson

Sinclair Lewis wrote into *Arrowsmith* so much of his basic personality that the novel is central to the revelation of the man and his work. Fortunately there is much material at hand pertaining to the genesis of the book; and the opportunity to trace the development of the characters and especially to note a multitude of editorial revisions and the reconstitution of sectional terminations was greatly expanded when, in the midst of his work, Lewis revised the still uncompleted book-manuscript for initial publication as a serial in the *Designer and the Woman's Magazine* from June 1924 through April 1925. The editors of the *Designer* also excised a great many passages throughout the manuscript; thus a study of editorial policy may easily be made.

Both Lewis and Paul Henry de Kruif have written of the dramatic origin of *Arrowsmith.* They had first met in the summer of 1922 "in the office of Dr. Morris Fishbein, of the *Journal of the American Medical Association,*" and that evening, during an ardent discussion on medical education, Lewis declared his resolution to write a story of a doctor who, "starting out as a competent general practitioner, emerges as a real scientist, despising ordinary 'success.' " Dr. de Kruif, bacteriologist, fresh from the laboratories of the Rockefeller Institute for Medical Research, agreed to help him. Together they "wandered from Barbados to Panama to Europe;...spent hours in laboratories in Panama, in London, in Paris," and "got in five to seven hours of work daily."

From *Twentieth Century Interpretations of* Arrowsmith, edited by Robert J. Griffin, © 1968 by Prentice-Hall, Inc., Englewood Cliffs, New Jersey.

Lewis typed, with "maps, books, diagrams and paper around him," including Patrick Manson's *Tropical Diseases;* de Kruif instructed him on medical and scientific matters, microbes, and the "lore of laboratories." Especially memorable to de Kruif was the hot Sunday afternoon on San Lucia when they let their imaginations play on a hypothetical sweep of the bubonic plague over the island, which Lewis later developed into a major section of the novel, and he reported that Lewis, "on the surface restless, hasty of temper, genial, . . . is patient, precise and accurate when he sits down to his typewriter." Lewis worked over a year on the novel in London and Fontainebleau.

The Lewis Collection in the Yale University Library contains many maps, diagrams, and notes that Lewis characteristically made to assist him in developing and visualizing a novel. For *Arrowsmith* he created imaginary maps for his Pony River Valley and the town of Wheatsylvania in North Dakota, and for the campus of the medical school of the University of Winnemac, as well as detailed drawings of the first, second, and third floors of the main medical building, the first and second floors of the anatomy building, and the thirtieth floor of the McGurk Building, the two top floors of which housed the McGurk Institute of Biology. Lewis also made a chronology of the life of Martin Arrowsmith and noted a long list of possible titles for the book. Such tentative titles as *The Stumbler* and *The Barbarian* clearly indicate certain qualities with which Lewis wished to endow Arrowsmith in "this biography of a young man who was in no degree a hero, who regarded himself as a seeker after truth yet who stumbled and slid back all his life and bogged himself in every obvious morass." He narrowed the list until the title became *Dr. Martin Arrowsmith* in the serialized version, and finally simply *Arrowsmith* in the American edition, Lewis noting of Arrowsmith that *"it's his personal and scientific career that counts much more than his medical career."*

In an italicized prefatory note in the book edition of *Arrowsmith,* Lewis generously recognized the service of de Kruif "for his realization of the characters as living people, for his philosophy as a scientist," and for supplying considerable "lore" of laboratories and medical and scientific institutions. In response to a letter of inquiry, Dr. de Kruif has assured the author of this article that part of the origin of Gottlieb—something of his nature and devotion to research—springs from Dr. de Kruif's acquaintance with Dr. Jacques Loeb, who was head of the Division of General Physiology of the Rockefeller Institute, and with Dr. Frederick George Novy, then Professor of Bacteriology and later

Dean of the School of Medicine of the University of Michigan, with whom Dr. de Kruif was associated for a decade; further, the McGurk Institute in *Arrowsmith* would not have been so vividly presented if Dr. de Kruif had not been associated recently with the Rockefeller Institute. Yet the principal characters are definitely and chiefly Lewis's creations and partake of his own character.

Arrowsmith is largely a projection of Lewis's own personality. Instinctively Lewis gave the title "The Death of Arrowsmith" to an autobiographical sketch originally published in *Coronet,* July 1, 1941, seventeen years after the publication of the novel in serialized form. And quite seriously in "Self-Portrait" (Berlin, August 1927), two years after the publication of the book, while it was still a sharply emotional memory, he identified certain of his own aspirations with Max Gottlieb and much of his own "loyalty to love" with Leora Tozer. Lewis here expressed it thus:

> There is really no Sinclair Lewis about whom even that diligent scribbler himself could write, outside of what appears in his characters. All his respect for learning, for integrity, for accuracy, and for the possibilities of human achievement are to be found not in the rather hectic and exaggerative man as his intimates see him, but in his portrait of Professor Max Gottlieb, in *Arrowsmith.* Most of the fellow's capacity for loyalty to love and friendship has gone into Leora in that same novel.

As for Sondelius, Lewis stated in "Self-Portrait" (Nobel Foundation), written in 1930 as an autobiographical sketch for the foundation five years after the book had appeared, that he had made "Gustaf Sondelius, of *Arrowsmith,* a Swede—and to me, Dr. Sondelius is the favorite among all my characters." This elevation of Sondelius to the "favorite" status is of psychological interest, even though it undoubtedly was done on the spur of the moment when Lewis was thinking of his relation to Swedes while writing to the Nobel Foundation. It comes as a bit of a surprise to readers, for Sondelius does not hold a truly prominent place in the novel. Mentioned first on page 171 of the 448-page novel, he does not enter in person until pages 182–85, and he does not appear again until page 336, when Lewis takes time to describe him "as possessing a little of Gottlieb's perception, something of Dad Silva's steady kindliness, something of Terry's tough honesty though none of his scorn of amenities, and with a spicy, dripping richness altogether his own." Therefore he becomes Arrowsmith's assistant, and Lewis chooses him to accompany Martin and Leora to the island of St. Hubert, where he destroys rats and handles official matters relative to the inoculation of the populace during the next twenty-five pages, and dies of the plague, sixty-seven pages before the end of the book. Actually, Lewis had drawn Sondelius with the sketchiness of an author creating a puppet of some stature for use in the machinery of a novel, and the character does not become a true creation. Yet Sondelius can be envisioned as possessing most of Gottlieb's integrity without his irascibility, and most of Arrowsmith's devotion to a scientific venture without his somewhat persistent immaturity and lack of balance or ability to be a moderator among men. Thinking of this, Lewis could, on the impulse of the moment, crown Sondelius "the favorite among all my characters," a figure having certain strengths lacking in Arrowsmith and Gottlieb, both of whom more closely partake of Lewis's own personality.

II

On October 10, 1923, while Lewis was in Europe working on *Arrowsmith,* Alfred Harcourt, his close friend and publisher, in a letter to "Red," reported a telephone call by Sewell Haggard, who told Harcourt that the Butterick people wanted to publish a feature serial during the next year to put the *Designer* "on the map," and he wished to inquire about the availability of a novel he had heard Lewis was finishing. Harcourt replied, "Do you want $50,000 worth?" Thus began a course of negotiations leading to the publication of *Dr. Martin Arrowsmith* in the *Designer.*

Lewis's reply from London on November 6 is significant and characteristic in its insistence that there be no compromise in the nature of the story if it should appear in the *Designer:*

> One thing I wish to emphasize. I suppose Haggard will have to cut, but I will not change the thing into a sunny sweet tale nor will I permit him to. *Does he understand that?* Please let me know, for otherwise he can't have it at any price. (Not that there's much really *offensive* in the novel, anyway. He needn't worry.)

Again from London, on November 12, Lewis reiterated his stand: "As I asked before, does Haggard understand there will be no sunny conventionalities tucked in?"

Lewis's fears proved groundless. Indeed, the arrangement for serial publication was most fortunate in all ways. He received a handsome price from the *Designer;* he enjoyed the extra time given him to develop the book; and, instinctively a journalist, he himself eliminated many scattered short passages which he still felt to be of value in the book but recognized as surplusage in serial form. From London on December 27, 1923, he wrote to Harcourt:

> If I were you (and in this case the you refers to everybody connected with Harcourt-Brace) I don't believe I'd even read the installments that go over to Haggard *because* I am more or less cutting from the book-manuscript for serial use—cutting out bits of philosophy which will (I think) be of considerable value in the book and little or none in the magazine. Wait till about the end of April, and you'll have the whole book ms. When I come home we can at leisure go over the book ms. and—this will be splendid—I can lay it away for several months and go over the whole thing again just before you start setting, a year or so from now.

The story progressed well. From London, February 9, 1924, he wrote Harcourt that in "about four days" he would be sending another 25,000 words to Haggard, who had cabled regarding the first 40,000 words: "Story splendid"; and on March 4, in another letter to Harcourt, he was sufficiently elated to remark that Haggard had said that "if the whole novel is up to the first 40,000 words, it will be the best thing I have ever done." Actually, Lewis quite realized that different media required different techniques. Not only did he understand the problems of popular journals, for which he had written, but he was thinking of the possibility of a screen version, which Sidney Howard eventually did for a Samuel Goldwyn production, starring Ronald Colman as Arrowsmith and Helen Hayes as Leora, to Lewis's satisfaction; and when Howard adapted *Dodsworth* for the stage, Lewis praised the playwright most enthusiastically, noting that though by reason of the medium the book had been radically changed in detail, the adapter did "preserve, and in the different milieu of the stage sincerely present, the real theme and characters of the story."

The depth of Lewis's interest in the medical and scientific "philosophy" of *Arrowsmith,* his personal willingness to start a controversy, and his faith in advertising are revealed in his letter to Harcourt from

Paris, December 27, 1924. *"And,"* he wrote, "besides the individual doctors, the editors of medical journals, the A.M.A. officials, and the college bacteriologists, *have Paul* [de Kruif] make out a list of other scientists to whom it should go in advance"; and he further suggested sending copies to other medical men, "e.g. [Abraham] Flexner," of the Carnegie Foundation for the Advancement of Teaching, who might not like it "quite as much as those who will." No changes in the text in the *Designer* affect Lewis's remarks on science, medicine, or medical institutions and those associated with them.

III

Scattered throughout the 448 pages of *Arrowsmith* in book form there are 336 complete paragraphs, long and short, not in the *Designer,* and there are at least 103 paragraphs which have been reduced approximately one to three lines and 59 paragraphs which have been cut four to 14 lines. There are only 26 complete paragraphs unique to the *Designer* and 37 paragraphs to which additions or substitutions were made. It is evident that for purposes of serialization the manuscript was fully and carefully edited without mutilating the fundamental scenes and theme. Indeed, it can well be argued that the story really lost little in the serial form and in many ways was improved by deletions of words and sentences which merely belabored the ideas or were blatant Lewisian expletives and obtrusive, derisive remarks.

Lewis's natural impulse was to be climactic, and *Arrowsmith* is a series of many short, dramatic scenes. Therefore, in spite of the hundreds of textual changes, no structural alterations were necessary to achieve a climax for each installment in the *Designer;* one was always conveniently at hand, at the end of either a chapter or a section within a chapter. Each of the eleven installments closes at a moment of high interest: when Martin goes home "engaged to two girls at once"; when Martin and his bride Leora are separated on their bridal night by her father; when Gottlieb at a crucial moment accepts a position with the McGurk Institute of Biology; when Leora's unborn baby is taken "from her, dead," and she and Martin, "eternally understanding," gaze "in the prairie twilight"; when Leora demands of Martin that he stop flirting with Orchid, and he determines to be successful at Nautilus; when Martin resolves to "make myself succeed" as Director of Public Health at Nautilus; when Martin energetically begins his researches at the McGurk Institute; when it is determined that Martin and Sondelius will go to the island of St. Hubert; when Martin, "aghast" at his beginning to fall in love with Joyce Lanyon, is "suddenly . . . out of bed, kneeling, praying to Leora"; when Martin jubilantly resolves to work with Terry at any cost on the action of derivatives of quinine on bacteria; when Martin, resting at evening with Terry in a boat, looks happily forward to further researches in quinine for two or three years, oblivious of home or position. What more in the way of dramatic structure could an editor of a popular journal demand for $50,000?

But though alterations in structure were not necessary, there were many attitudes, ideas, explosions of satirical invective, and uncouth expressions that did need attention and excision. One was the minor problem of expletives. Lewis was opposed to "obscenity" in writing. In "Obscenity and Obscurity" he stated: "I don't like the use, either in a book or in the parlor, the use of any of those Nine Saxon Monosyllables which the sly and the roughneck use to describe natural functions just to be spicy." But expletives such as *damn, hell,* and *by God* were normal with Lewis. He peppered *Arrowsmith* with them whenever he thought Martin (and occasionally some other character) would use them in moments of passion, exultation, or moral indignation. They were omitted or altered in the *Designer* without loss to the story; indeed, the story was improved. The reader's general liking and respect for Martin are enhanced by omissions which actually do not diminish his impetuosity or convictions.

Nor could the *Designer* find virtue in certain of the remarks of Lewis rising from his natural satirical bent and his indignation at moral smugness. These remarks occasionally took the form of mere buzzing and stinging at random, including the mention of religious affiliations in a derogatory way. Lewis recognized this limitation of his powers of precision in expressing his true feeling. In "Self-Portrait" (Berlin, August 1927) he wrote: "Why, this man, still so near to being an out and out Methodist or Lutheran . . . , is so infuriated by ministers who . . . keep from ever admitting publicly their confusing doubts that he risks losing all the good friends he once had among the ministers by the denunciations in *Elmer Gantry,*" and the strong satirical strain in him continually cost him friendships throughout his life. He was essentially lonely.

Throughout *Arrowsmith* there is no favorable response to religious institutions or to persons affiliated with them; Lewis's sympathy is reserved for only one man with conscientious convictions about religion—Sondelius, the sincere agnostic. Lewis's remarks in this area are frequently omitted in the *Designer,* and the deletions reveal the distinctions in attitude between him and the editorial principles governing the magazine. . . .

As a novel mixed with satire and sympathy, *Arrowsmith* is peopled with characters subjectively drawn for a purpose. They stand as revelations of Lewis's responses toward different types of men. They are characters whom he despised or admired, creatures endowed either with characteristics he detested or with energy and ideals and foibles he could treat sympathetically and with understanding. As Martin Arrowsmith and Gustaf Sondelius and Max Gottlieb are of his own blood, they have both virtues and limitations. In contrast to these, for example, there is Angus Duer, the cool, self-centered valedictorian medical student who becomes a capable surgeon with an eye to wealth, and who keeps in good physical trim, allowing himself "only one drink daily." Lewis somewhat envied Duer's capabilities, yet he despised him with a hate so deep that he unnecessarily, perhaps unbelievably for the readers, made him mentally a murderer. But in general there is a mixture of strengths and weaknesses in Lewis's characters, though some of the weaknesses occasionally seem to have been gratuitously bestowed on them by the author rather than being necessarily inherent. The version of *Arrowsmith* in the *Designer* omits a number of the grosser attributes. Sometimes the omissions show an unwarranted regard for the sensibilities of the readers, sometimes the omissions relieve the story of paragraphs which merely belabor issues and impede the flow of the narrative, and sometimes they clear the text of rather unjustifiable satirical angularities. . . .

In his desire to portray Martin Arrowsmith realistically as a young man possessed of rather grave faults, Lewis gave him emotional characteristics which the *Designer* excised; and he also described brief scenes in the relationship of Martin with Madeline Fox, Orchid Pickerbaugh, and his two wives, Leora Tozer and Joyce Lanyon, which the *Designer* removed without harming the theme of the novel. While Martin is paying his attentions to Madeline Fox before his marriage to Leora Tozer, the *Designer* does not allow Martin to be characterized as a young man who, though not a Don Juan, was nevertheless one of whom it could not be said that his "intentions. . . were what is called 'honorable.'. . . He wanted—like most poor and ardent young men in such a case, he wanted all he could get." When Martin and Leora enter her parents' home after the elopement, the readers are not too clearly informed that Mr. Tozer orders his daughter to her own room alone; there is no statement that they "would in no way, uh, act as though they were married till he gave permission," or that, as for Martin, "that was his bridal night; tossing in his bed, ten yards from her.". . . .

Lewis's dominant motive in writing *Arrowsmith* was to extol the truly professional spirit in medical teaching and research, and to expose all intruding chicanery, greed, egotism, and ignorance. So as a satirist he and de Kruif endowed the McGurk Institute and some of its men with characteristics he wished to pillory. He struck out boldly, often mockingly, and some of his remarks were excised from the *Designer.* . . .

Certain medical diseases and references are omitted from the *Designer* in deference to the feelings—or the supposed feelings—of its feminine readers. The excision of these items does somewhat weaken the impact of the story, though in a few instances the omissions lighten Lewis's too heavy hand. For example, Lewis overworked references to the Wassermann test in the book, and this test is entirely excised for the *Designer.* During the illness of Leora in pregnancy, Arrowsmith, in the *Designer,* does not denounce "Nature for her way of tricking human beings, by every gay device of moonlight and white limbs and reaching loneliness, into having babies, then making birth as cruel and clumsy and wasteful as she could." And either Lewis or the editor of the *Designer* did not care to publish in the magazine the whole section dealing with Martin's suffering from neurasthenia: the readers never learn that for a short time he read subway posters backwards, feared darkness, thought that burglars might be about, felt the "cord of an assassin squeezing his throat," and drifted into anthropophobia and siderodromophobia.

Associated with these passages are a few others excised from the *Designer* as probably being too repulsive for its readers. They are scenes which do add a certain power to the book, but they are strongly grotesque. . . .

The text of the *Designer* lacks a number of facts and also a number of jabs at persons and concepts which any satirist has a right to include, but which are extraneous Lewisian comments not well woven into the fabric of the story. . . .

There are, finally, a number of excisions made solely to shorten the novel for serialization, and the absence of these passages need not be lamented. Typical examples are the description of Loizeau operating at a clinic, much of the early life of Gottlieb, some of the bustling activities of Arrowsmith at the McGurk Institute while engaged in research, certain of the passages elaborating Gottlieb's tribulations as Director of the McGurk Institute, a quotation from a scientific paper read by Arrowsmith, and the visits of the social set to Martin's laboratory.

IV

The passages that appear in the *Designer* but not in the book are of two types: they are slight alterations inserted to fill lacunae made by the excision of text in the book not appearing in the *Designer,* or they are passages which Lewis may have discarded in the process of revising his manuscript to improve the novel in book form. There are many slight changes, and nine places where one or more paragraphs are to be found only in the *Designer.* . . .

There are many references to alcoholic drinks both in the book and in the *Designer,* and some of the references in the book are not in the magazine; but, oddly enough, there also are some other references in the *Designer* which are not in the book. Only in the *Designer* the chief steward sends up a bottle of Scotch, Sondelius invents "a drink made chiefly of cognac and Grand Marnier," the governor gives Arrowsmith a glass of Napoleon brandy, Sondelius proposes "a drink at the Ice House" and has too many "planter's punches," Terry suggests that Martin come to his room for a drink, Martin and Terry have a drink from "Roger Lanyon's ancestral stock," and Joyce mentions Martin's "many whiskey sodas." Lewis probably recognized that he had overloaded his story with drinks beyond excuse or occasion for them.

Lewis encountered no difficulty in writing of the courtship and married life of Martin and Leora; he breathed life into them. But he could not well portray the prenuptial and nuptial life of Martin and Joyce; he could not bring these scenes fully to life. He must have sensed this failure, for there are three passages in the thirty-seventh chapter which are in the *Designer* but were cut out or revised in the book. . . .

V

No reader may doubt that three purposes possessed Lewis's mind as he wrote *Arrowsmith:* to give full allegiance to scientists wholly devoted to basic research in medicine, to satirize those in medical research who are not truly dedicated to their profession, and to tell a story of young love as realistically and sympathetically as he could.

The fact that his novels have not retained their full popular impact is to some degree the common fate of works of satirists that bear the date and seal of their generation in aura and manner. To each age its own satirical tone, its impulse to rewrite history. With the passage of time, certain limitations of Lewis's literary skill and the more angular characteristics of his satire become readily discernible. In *Arrowsmith,* emphasis is sought too frequently by the simple device of expletives. Hypocrisy, selfishness, mediocrity, and smallness of mind of persons in colleges, churches, the medical profession, and medical research institutions too frequently are satirized with the petulant impatience of a zealot unarmed by humor. The mature reader is bothered not only by the many climaxes, some of which are artificial, but by the tyranny of the author over his characters. Scorn and ridicule often make visible the strings leading from most of the characters to the manipulating hands of the author.

These limitations are less noticeable in the version edited for the *Designer.* Although the many climaxes that Lewis contrived for his effects are more conspicuous in the *Designer* than in the book, and although the few paragraphs deleted from the *Designer* revisions are to the advantage of the book, most of the many deletions made for the *Designer* removed irritating blemishes. Even the omission of the non-satirical expository passages lessens our sense of Lewis's domination over his characters; Gottlieb seems the more real when commentary is reduced. Lewis and the editor of the *Designer* improved the story, though the author, in his eagerness to challenge hypocrisy and mediocrity, would not believe it.

The Ambivalence towards Romance

Martin Light

Lewis admired the laboratory researcher and made use of much of the researcher's method in his extensive and careful fieldwork and note-taking as preparation for his novels. Research would restrain the idler's fantasizing. Furthermore, the researcher is both objectively removed from life and ultimately useful to it. Lewis feared being useless: not the idle but the industrious apprentice was he, not the dilettante or bohemian but the eight-hours-a-day professional writer. Hard work was the pioneer way, and whatever reading, thinking, dreaming young Lewis had needed to do—though they might look to his townspeople like time-wasting—were but the prelude to the hard and useful labor which would follow. These fears and justifications became a credo, declared in 1921. Though overblown, pretentious, and even embarrassing to read, it is an important statement of his attitude:

> The builder, and he may be a builder in business as much as in any art, concentrates on his building, yet sees all of life expanding, as circle beyond circle of possible achievement is disclosed. He will neither whine, "I can't find time," nor, at the other extreme, will he pound his own back and bellow, "Oh, I'm one grand little worker." His idol is neither the young man sighing over a listless pipe, nor the human calliope. He works, persistently, swiftly, without jar.

Not the least interesting phrase here is the one which suggests that art can be "built." But of greater importance in the credo is the rapid

From *The Quixotic Vision of Sinclair Lewis.* © 1975 Purdue University Press by Purdue Research Foundation, West Lafayette, Indiana.

evocation of certain character types. Neither a whiner nor a bellower be; much of Lewis's satirical characterization is an excoriation of whiners and bellowers, who appear as bohemians, preachers, and salesmen. Such types arose to the front of his consciousness from his experience of life—in the village, at Yale, on a cattleboat to England, in a socialistic utopian community, in Greenwich Village, in the offices of New York publishing houses. To oppose them, Lewis drew portraits of the "builders"—engineers and architects—some of whom he tried as best he could to make significantly alert to circles of meaningful achievement. If the voice of one human being echoes within him, it surely must be that of his conscientious and puritanical father, the man who worked hard and always paid his debts.

While still working on *Babbitt,* Lewis wrote his publisher that he was planning to make his next novel "not satiric at all; rebellious as ever, perhaps, but the central character *heroic.*" He added that he was already getting gleams for it. What he was specifically getting gleams for was the labor novel which he never wrote. Instead, he wrote *Arrowsmith,* which was the result of a meeting he had soon afterward with Dr. Paul de Kruif in which Lewis recognized at once that the story of a medical researcher offered, in a way congenial to him, the kind of heroic material he had been seeking.

While he worked on *Arrowsmith,* Lewis was more enthusiastic than he had ever been before: "I am quite sure that it will be much better than either *Main St* or *Babbitt;* the characters have more life to me, more *stir.*" He said that he thought the new book would be the meatiest of all, in respect to character, places, contrasting purposes and views of life. It was also the novel into which Lewis felt he had put the best of himself. All his "respect for learning, for integrity, for accuracy, and for the possibilities of human achievement," he said, were to be found in the portrait of Professor Max Gottlieb. And most of his "capacity for loyalty to love and friendship" had gone into the character of Leora Tozer, Arrowsmith's wife. Elsewhere Lewis said that Dr. Sondelius was the favorite among all his characters. Finally the identification of himself with Dr. Martin Arrowsmith—physician and bacteriological researcher—is symbolized in Lewis's title of a mock obituary of himself: "The Death of Arrowsmith."

Arrowsmith, like most of Lewis's other novels, is a tale of a quixote. From the opening, Martin Arrowsmith is a wanderer, a fancifier, a romantic. He searches for the commonsense aspect of himself, for some outward figures who can encourage his control over romance and keep him at his work, and for a basis upon which to criticize those fools, clowns, hypocrites, and exploiters he encounters in various heroic engagements. The material out of which Arrowsmith's mind and values were created is that of popular fiction.

Judging from the otherwise unnecessary opening section to the book, it appears as if Lewis took very seriously his intention to give the story broad heroic, perhaps mythic, scope. The spirit of Arrowsmith had pioneer sources. We see his great-grandmother, a ragged girl of fourteen, crossing the country on a wagon, her father sick, her mother dead, and her younger brothers and sisters clamoring about her. The old man says, "Ye better turn." "We're going on," she replies with pioneer courage, "jus' long as we can. Going West! They's a whole lot of new things I aim to be seeing!" She is on the road; she seeks adventure: she suggests the union of the metaphors of the quixote and the pioneer.

In addition to pioneer ancestry, Arrowsmith possesses an epic blood-line: German, French, Scotch, Irish, Spanish, a mixture Lewis labels "Jewish," and a great deal of English, "which is itself a combination of Primitive Britain, Celt, Phoenician, Roman, German, Dane, and Swede." Arrowsmith's parentage is shrouded like that of the hero of tradition; his father and mother neither appear nor are ever talked of nor remembered by the son.

It is not from family that Arrowsmith learns the values of life, but from three mentors—Doc Vickerson, Max Gottlieb, and Terry Wickett. The first mentor appears only in chapter 1. There is a fuss made about a symbolic gift of a "beloved magnifying glass" that Doc gives to Arrowsmith, but the glass is never recalled thereafter. Yet it is significant that the Arrowsmith who has pioneer blood in his veins should begin his quest with inspiration from Lewis's typically American pariah, the defeated bachelor-drunkard-agnostic who is nevertheless keen, inquiring, independent. Soon enough Vickerson is supplanted by Professor Gottlieb, both more brilliant and more filled with doubt. As a Jew and a European, he is trying to find his way in an alien culture. Lastly, from Wickett, the representative of the new scientific yet cynical vigor of America, Arrowsmith learns how to escape from the frustrations of society to a primitive sanctuary in nature. In this novel, then, we come to Lewis's attempt to create a hero—that is (in Caroline Gordon's words), a person who answers some call to action, who seems to unite and portray certain trends of his age. It is a quixotic hero that Lewis creates, but one not any the less representative for all that.

Although the reader should not lose sight of the book's pretentious beginnings, soon a human story unfolds. Lewis speaks of Arrowsmith, not as a giant, but as a young man "who regarded himself as a seeker after truth yet who stumbled and slid back all his life and bogged himself in every obvious morass." Now on this level we have the man of science as essentially an ordinary man, plain, simple, unintellectual, and bungling, "full of hasty faults and of perverse honesty; a young man often unkindly, often impolite." But he had one gift—his curiosity.

We are not given lengthy book lists that suggest how reading has affected Arrowsmith's mind, but we see some later book choices that tell us what kinds of reading he has an affinity for. Arrowsmith is but half-educated, we are told. To remedy the defect, he reads Robert Service, European history, *The Golden Bowl* ("which an unfortunate schoolteacher had left"), and Conrad, from whom he feeds his fancy (as we might expect), not his moral being: "As [Arrowsmith] drove the prairie roads, he was marching into jungle villages—sun helmets, orchids, lost temples of obscene and dog-faced deities, secret and sun-scarred rivers." During the miseries of the pregnancy of his wife Leora, to soothe their troubled minds "he read to her, not history now and Henry James but 'Mrs. Wiggs of the Cabbage Patch,' which both of them esteemed a very fine tale."

Yet later in New York, Arrowsmith reads "the classics of physical science: Copernicus and Galileo, Lavoisier, Newton, LaPlace, Descartes, Faraday. He became completely bogged in Newton's 'Fluxions.' " Are these names just amusing counters for Lewis? The books seem to make little impression upon his hero. Furthermore, at no point in the progress of the novel does Arrowsmith's manner of speaking change; always it is the talk of an exuberant boy. To the pregnant Leora he says soothingly, "Golly, we—No, not 'golly.' Well, what *can* you say except 'golly'?" and he goes on to promise travel to "Italy and all those places. All those old narrow streets and old castles! There must be scads of 'em."

The novel is laced with quixotism beyond the castles of Italy. Arrowsmith declares his quixotic intentions at the outset: "I'm going to have them all"—fame, women, adventure (he will "see the world"). One summer, when he is working as a telephone lineman, he has a vision:

He was atop a pole and suddenly, for no clear cause, his eyes opened and he saw; as though he had just awakened he saw that the prairie was vast, that the sun was kindly on rough pasture and ripening wheat, on the old horses, the easy, broad-beamed, friendly horses, and on his red-faced jocose companions; he saw that the meadow larks were jubilant, and blackbirds shining by little pools, and with the living sun all life was living.

His girlfriend, Madeline Fox, seems a sister of Carol Kennicott in her own fancying: "She compared her refuge to the roof of a Moorish palace, to a Spanish patio, to a Japanese garden, to a 'pleasaunce of old Provençal.' "

Then Lewis, the fantasist, takes flight. Arrowsmith meets Leora Tozer, who will become his bride shortly. There is a rhapsodic passage during their first meeting:

> Sound of mating birds, sound of spring blossoms dropping in the tranquil air, the bark of sleepy dogs at midnight; who is to set them down and make them anything but hackneyed? And as natural, as conventional, as youthfully gauche, as eternally beautiful and authentic as those ancient sounds was the talk of Martin and Leora in that passionate half-hour when each found in the other a part of his own self, always vaguely missed, discovered now with astonished joy. They rattled like hero and heroine of a sticky tale, like sweatshop operatives, like bouncing rustics, like prince and princess.

After being dismissed from the university, Arrowsmith takes to wandering:

> Always, in America, there remains from pioneer days a cheerful pariahdom of shabby young men who prowl causelessly from state to state, from gang to gang, in the power of the Wanderlust. They wear black sateen shirts, and carry bundles. They are not permanently tramps. They have home towns to which they return, to work quietly in the factory or the section-gang for a year—for a week—and as quietly to disappear again. . . . Into that world of voyageurs Martin vanished.

Furthermore as an intern he is involved in soap opera episodes like the one in which he attends to the victims of a fire: "They heard the blang-blang-blang of a racing ambulance, incessant, furious, defiant. Without orders, the crowd opened, and through them, almost grazing them, slid the huge gray car. At the back, haughty in white uniform, nonchalant on a narrow seat, was The Doctor—Martin Arrowsmith." He rushes to an unconscious youngster who has inhaled too much smoke. A reporter approaches Arrowsmith. " 'Will he pull through, Doc?' he twanged. 'Sure, I think so. Suffocation. Heart's still going.' Martin yelped the last words from the step at the back of the ambulance."

But whatever Lewis shows us in dialogue and action, his exposition insists upon Arrowsmith's growth and maturity. "While Martin developed in a jagged way from the boy of Wheatsylvania to mature man, his relations to Leora developed from loyal boy-and-girl adventurousness to lasting solidity." Yet shortly thereafter we read, "He was sobbing, with her head on his shoulder, 'Oh, you poor, scared, bullied kid, trying to be grownup.' " Can we overlook the slick-magazine language of such passages? I think not. Here is a section in which Arrowsmith diverts himself with Orchid Pickerbaugh, aged nineteen: "One day when Orchid came swarming all over the laboratory and perched on the bench with a whisk of stockings, he stalked to her, masterfully seized her wrists, and kissed her as she deserved to be kissed." He is at once frightened; she is shocked. "He kissed her again. She yielded and for a moment there was nothing in the universe."

This novel, with its serious theme, has been acclaimed as Lewis's best work. Nevertheless, in view of the passages which I have been examining and the protagonist who is emerging from them, I find its heroic pretension embarrassing, unless the hero be thought of as a quixote. Otherwise, one episode after another of the book "freezes up our credulity and provokes our fiercest denial," as Allen Tate has said of another novel. In New York, when Arrowsmith hits upon something significant, we are shown his frenzy and exhaustion as he rushes to consult the library, as he experiments, as he takes notes, neglects Leora, ignores even his weariness. His language at such moments is impulsive and chaotic. He forgets Gottlieb's advice to be calm. "God, woman, I've got it! The real big stuff! I've found something, not a chemical you put in I mean, that eats bugs—dissolves 'em—kills 'em. May be a big new step in therapeutics. Oh, no, rats, I don't suppose it really is. Prob'ly just another of my bulls." He sobs to Leora, "Oh, I couldn't do anything without you! Don't ever leave me! I do love you so, even if this damned work does keep me tied up." He becomes sick with nervous exhaustion. He is never far from hysteria. If medical researchers do not in fact act so wildly, as one commentator will argue later, many readers were apparently swept up by Lewis's picture of the hero at work.

Nowhere is Arrowsmith so confused, so innocent, and so idealistic as in his relationships with women; in this regard, as in the bent of his mind toward science, he is indeed a spiritual offspring of such quixotes as Hawk Ericson and Milt Daggett. By the writing of this book, Lewis has altered his ideas about women, however. He had found sinister elements in the eager young feminists who wished only for self-realization. They had metamorphosed from the idealized Ruth Winslow and Claire Boltwood, from the more determined Una Golden, into the nervously reformist and uncertain Carol Kennicott. By *Arrowsmith* Lewis was bitterly portraying women he called "Improvers."

Arrowsmith becomes involved with four women who reflect important aspects of the novel's message: Madeline Fox, Leora Tozer, Orchid Pickerbaugh, and Joyce Lanyon. Lewis gathers the good qualities of women into the much-admired portrait of Leora Tozer. To Orchid Pickerbaugh he ascribes immature frivolity. He displays shallow pretension, finickiness and uselessness in Madeline Fox and Joyce Lanyon. By the time he wrote *Arrowsmith,* Lewis had become so antagonistic to such "princesses" as Ruth and Claire that he could editorialize that "few women can for long periods keep from trying to Improve their men, and to Improve means to change a person from what he is, whatever that may be, into something else." Such women cannot be restrained. Young Arrowsmith falls in love with Madeline, who is an Improver. But shortly thereafter he meets one of the few women in Lewis's fiction who are not Improvers—the most praised women in all of Lewis's books, the compliant, self-effacing, and loyal Leora Tozer. With her, Arrowsmith felt "an instant and complete comradeship. . . free from the fencing and posing of his struggle with Madeline." Leora "was full of laughter at humbugs." Futhermore, "she was feminine but undemanding; she was never Improving and rarely shocked."

Arrowsmith finds himself engaged to both girls. An important choice must be made between the Improver and the Companion. To demonstrate the differences, Lewis arranges a scene in which Arrowsmith naively and quixotically brings the two girls together. Madeline reacts badly (for which, if for nothing else, she ought to be excused—it's a rather foolish thing the hero does, though it is indicative of Lewis's sense of romantic drama); she stalks out. Leora understands and remains.

But the spirit of Madeline the Improver does not leave the story. It returns in the body of Joyce Lanyon some 315 pages later. During the plague episode, Arrowsmith encounters Joyce, whom he sees as his transforming vision must. She must be his sister, he thinks. "She was perhaps thirty to his thirty-seven, but in her slenderness, her paleness, her black brows and dusky hair, she was his twin; she was his self enchanted." Arrowsmith's analysis is faulty, however, the result of his ever-active fancy. Joyce revives the spirit of Madeline. Yet after Leora dies of the plague, Arrowsmith marries Joyce. With plenty of time and opportunity to observe her, Arrowsmith walks straight into marriage with an Improving Woman: "An Arranger and even an Improver was Joyce," we are told by the author before the marriage occurs, and we readers have no information about Joyce that is unknown to the hero. She declares to him, "I do like pretty people and gracious manners and good games." She is a woman who likes to play; she says so. But there is an important difference to note in the author's treatment of the matter here. At this point in his development, play has unpleasant connotations. The notion of play has become attached to the Arranger, the Improver, the Nag. This attitude, which had begun to appear in the treatment of Carol Kennicott, who had the urge to improve the town, is fully formulated in Joyce Lanyon. From this point on, women who want to play do not receive the author's sympathy.

Joyce and her kind contrast with Leora, who obeyed Arrowsmith's wishes and understood "without his saying them all the flattering things he planned to say." But not so with Joyce: "She could, she said, kill a man who considered her merely convenient furniture." "She expected him to remember her birthday, her taste in wine, her liking for flowers, and her objection to viewing the process of shaving. She wanted a room to herself; she insisted that he knock before entering." Arrowsmith believes that he has made himself the slave of Joyce. He decides to escape from her. With startling callousness, he leaves his son as well as Joyce herself. As he retreats to a shack in the Vermont woods, he kisses their infant son and mutters, "Come to me when you grow up, old man."

William Wrenn and Hawk Ericson each had a choice between two women. Now in *Arrowsmith* such a choice reemerges as an important element in the form of Lewis's books. Madeline Fox and Joyce Lanyon, standing at the opening and the close of the novel, can symbolize grasping and selfish impulses in our society, while Leora Tozer represents generous and considerate ones. Arrowsmith can do his best work only in the atmosphere of Leora, or alone. For Leora had borne the tedium of Arrowsmith's work without complaint. "She sat quiet (a frail child, only up to one's shoulder, not nine minutes older than at marriage, nine years before), or she napped inoffensively, in the long living-room of their flat, while he worked." But she does more than bear the tedium. Her baby dies, and one suspects that its death is a convenience that keeps Arrowsmith unburdened by responsibility. She overlooks his faults and indiscretions and never interferes with his work. Leora's death, which occurs by accident during the plague at St. Hubert, suggests that Lewis may have wished to lay an extra affliction upon Arrowsmith so that he will be forced to retreat from the world. Arrowsmith's remorse is silence; he displays no guilt at all, though he had abandoned her at a lodge on the island, where she contracts the disease. After her death, he marries Joyce. How slow to learn Lewis's male characters are! They seem to need one extra demonstration of truths they should know but somehow cannot accept—and this need for an extra demonstration causes an impatience with the structure of his books at the same time that it suggests some tragic overtones of the hero who cannot change. In *Main Street* and in *Arrowsmith*, as in *Dodsworth* and *Cass Timberlane*, which follow later, the extra demonstration, actually a repetition of something already clear to the reader, lengthens the book. Of the best work Lewis did, only *Babbitt* has no such repetition and only *Babbitt* is as tight a novel as any of the others might have been, to their benefit.

The theme of *Arrowsmith* is that the frauds, wastrels, and hypocrites of American life divert a man from his best, purest work and that his only salvation is retreat. There is no place for Arrowsmith in McGurk Institute or in Joyce's circle of friends, or anywhere else in America. This book is Lewis's most comprehensive testing of American environments. In its course Arrowsmith ventures across the nation, from the village of Wheatsylvania, North Dakota, to the small city of Nautilus, to the middle-sized midwestern city of Zenith, to Chicago, and to New York. Everywhere he is rejected and everywhere he rejects. Everywhere self-realization is stifled and idealism is defiled. He resolves these by withdrawal. To justify his retreat, Arrowsmith enunciates his code of the pioneers. He says that the objection that there is a responsibility to one's family has been what has kept "almost everybody, all these centuries, from being anything but a machine for digestion and propagation and obedience." Very few men ever "willingly leave a soft bed for a shanty bunk in order to be pure . . . and those of us that are pioneers—." He stops, and the word *pioneer* recalls not only the book's opening passages but one of Lewis's controlling ideas.

Carl Van Doren thought that "there is something true to an honored American tradition in Arrowsmith's retirement," something that reminded him of Daniel Boone and Leatherstocking. But Warren Beck, who finds Arrowsmith "a crude and lopsided human being," has said that this retreat which frees Arrowsmith "of feminine domination, social intrusions, or even any friction with colleagues" means that "the terms under which Arrowsmith succeeds are thus less significant, humanly speaking, than those under which Babbitt failed." Some readers believe, then, that Arrowsmith's retreat in the name of the pioneer spirit is but a further excuse for one of Lewis's boy-men never to mature. Bernard DeVoto, who said that "Martin suffers from arrested development" and "is a fool," noted further that "his customary state of mind while working at his trade has caused a bacteriologist of my acquaintance to want—I use his own winning expression—to puke." A Harvard bacteriologist has written: "If an epidemologist on a plague study talked and behaved in the manner of the hero of *Arrowsmith,* he would be regarded as something of a yellow ass and a nuisance by his associates."

Yet in the book there is also Gottlieb to uphold the ideal of the scientific attitude. In Gottlieb Lewis mixed dignity and genius and flaws in a more fully realized characterization. To Arrowsmith he had given nothing like Gottlieb's sense of sorrow nor his vision of the potential achievement of the human race nor his cynicism. Gottlieb has the task of expressing the themes of the book. It is he who voices the despair about the failures of human accomplishment. It is he who suggests that in the scientific approach lies the hope of the future. Significantly, Gottlieb makes no withdrawal from the world until his final illness, but continues his work in spite of heavy miseries which he suffers. Lewis surrounds Gottlieb in mystery. If Gottlieb is at the opening a fabulous and legendary character ("It was said that he could create life in the laboratory") and if Arrowsmith first sees him as "a tall figure, ascetic, self-contained, apart...unconscious of the world" and "romantic as a cloaked horseman," yet when Arrowsmith later comes to his office, he sees Gottlieb as "testy and middle-aged," with wrinkles, "a man who had headaches, who became agonizingly tired, who could be loved." Gottlieb is cynical about most of his students— they are "potatoes." But to some few students he can teach "the ultimate lesson of science, which is to wait and doubt." Arrowsmith becomes a disciple.

A two-chapter interlude in the history of Arrowsmith's career fills out the characterization of Gottlieb. His plans for a research institution lead to his dismissal from the University of Winnemac. He then

compromises his principles by taking a job with a commercial laboratory in Pittsburgh. In his misery Gottlieb turns to the Book of Job. Yet
although we are led inward, here as so often elsewhere Lewis's fanciful
notions mar the effect. Lewis imagines an unbelievable scene intended
to give breadth to his characterization by pushing it to outer limits;
instead, it interrupts the impact of his story. It seem that Gottlieb, "the
placidly virulent hater of religious rites, had a religious-seeming custom."
He would kneel by his bed and let his mind run free. "It was very much
like prayer, though certainly there was no formal invocation, no consciousness of a Supreme Being—other than Max Gottlieb." The episode seems extravagant when we find that the subject of his prayer is
"commercialism." Furthermore, there is nothing in *Job* nor in Jewish
religious observance that would lead Gottlieb to perform the rite which
Lewis reports to us—even taking fully into account that Gottlieb is not
a practicing Jew and might even intend an affront to orthodoxy. At
such crucial points in his characterization Lewis romanticizes. His re-
portorial technique fails to provide him with information; fabrication
takes over.

Gottlieb, in spite of his misery, succeeds in producing antitoxin in
the test tube. The head of the commercial laboratory pressures him to
give up verification and begin producing and marketing antitoxin at
once. Gottlieb's older daughter runs off with a gambler; his son is
worthless; his wife dies. It is a desperate moment. But suddenly and
fortunately the McGurk Institute in New York City calls him to join
its staff. At this point he leaves the novel for 132 pages. Then, having
read an article by Arrowsmith, Gottlieb invites him to join the institute. Gottlieb speaks a famous passage, his statement of the religion of
the scientist. The philanthropists, the doctors, the preachers, the man-
ufacturers, the eloquent statesmen, and soft-hearted authors have
made a mess of the world. "Maybe now it is time for the scientist, who
works and searches and never goes around howling how he loves
everybody!" Into this goes Lewis's Wellsian hope for salvation of the
world through science. Gottlieb's advice is "work twice as hard as you
can, and keep people from using you. I will try to protect you from
Success."

So inspired, Arrowsmith "prayed then the prayer of the scientist,"
a fantasy in inflated rhetoric, probably true to the character Lewis has
created but embarrassing to anyone listening over Arrowsmith's
shoulder: "God give me unclouded eyes and freedom from haste. God
give me a quiet and relentless anger against all pretense and all preten-

tious work and all work left slack and unfinished. God give me a restlessness whereby I may neither sleep nor accept praise till my observed results equal my calculated results or in pious glee I discover and assault my error. God give me strength not to trust to God!" Carl Van Doren found this prayer "Faustian" while Bernard DeVoto found it repulsive. It seems boyish, if nothing else, and it might have been created under the inspiration of Kipling's "If."

After Martin discovers phage, Gottlieb, true to his science, cautions him that further proof be sought. When it is revealed that phage has been discovered in Europe, Gottlieb helps soothe this disappointment. "Martin, it is nice that you will corroborate D'Hérelle. That is science: to work and not to care—too much—if somebody else gets the credit." This is the essence of Gottlieb's character and a deeper message than that of world-salvation through science. When Arrowsmith offers to test phage during a plague in St. Hubert, Gottlieb insists that he use the phage with only half the patients and keep the other as controls. Lewis adds a pathetic note to the departure: as Arrowsmith and his wife sail, they see Gottlieb at the pier, running to wave farewell, then, not finding them, turning sadly away. On his return to New York, Arrowsmith finds Gottlieb senile, unable to speak English, unable to recognize him. Arrowsmith had wanted forgiveness for the quixotic gesture of throwing over the scientific controls at St. Hubert and inoculating everyone so that he could not tell whether the serum had had any effect upon the subsiding of the plague. (Robert Morss Lovett wrote that the phenomena of the plague were sufficiently well known so that if all were inoculated and most survived, the cure *had* been found.) Lewis adds, "Martin understood that never could he be punished now and cleansed. Gottlieb had sunk into his darkness still trusting him."

I find *Arrowsmith* a test of our response to the quixotic novel. In spite of my reservations about this book, much of it is admirable. There are satiric passages of great skill. The handling of Wheatsylvania, which I shall not recount, shows that Lewis had become even more deft at satirizing villages than he was in the creation of Gopher Prairie. A large gallery of doctors is exposed. But Arrowsmith himself is an exhibit of the American who never grows up, whose escape from a manipulative woman and a crushing social system seems less than estimable because he will take no responsibility for his child nor show grief for the bride who had served him.

Whatever the defects of the book, the hold that it has upon its readers is the result of Lewis's great energy. *Arrowsmith* overflows with energy—adolescent as it may seem at times. Whether we are watching Arrowsmith ride the ambulance to a fire or shout his joy at discovering a cure for plague, we are swept up by an energy that cannot be dismissed—a dedication to hard work and a rage for justice that are Lewis's special brazen, audacious qualities. *Arrowsmith* requires only that Lewis have perceived his hero with irony, with Cervantine distance so that the quixotic qualities that we have noticed could be read as mock heroics. Carried away by the injunction to create a hero, Lewis withholds the comic perspective from Arrowsmith and asks us to take Arrowsmith's quixotic reading, adventures, and enchantments quite seriously.

One can see how Lewis strove to move onward from *Babbitt* to what he intended as a heroic novel. His protagonist would be a common man engaged in a large enterprise. Lewis's method of extravagant gestures, leading to the plague at St. Hubert, would give the novel and its questing hero their symbolic power. He did, in fact, achieve much. But our disappointments come at those places where Lewis called to his aid the very excesses of fancy which he ought to have mocked. Lewis seemed to be caught by his ambivalence toward romance at precisely that moment when he was realizing the fulfillment of his ambitions.

Three Max Gottliebs: Lewis's, Dreiser's, and Walker Percy's View of the Mechanist-Vitalist Controversy

Mary G. Land

The collapse of Sinclair Lewis's reputation has been exceeded only by the vagaries of Dreiser's. Critical articles on Lewis are noticeable by their paucity. Dreiser, on the other hand, is alternately sent to Coventry and resuscitated.

One clue to their downfall—in addition to the usual charges of overdocumentation, overtopicality, misapprehension of the nature of reality, and failure to explore multiple point of view—may be that Lewis and Dreiser achieved something rare in American literature: a reasonable facsimile of the scientific enterprise. Santayana credited the "literary psychology" with a horror of science, especially of mechanistic science, a "black art," dealing in unholy abstractions. To counter it the psychological fictionist (Santayana's example is Bergson) "keeps his metaphysical exorcisms and antidotes always at hand, to render it innocuous." Bergson's antidote was the *"elan vital,"* but all anti-mechanist doctrines insist upon the existence of some essential barrier between what is life and what is not life and upon the presence of some vital spark or force or principle to set what they think of as brute, inert matter going. It may be a neo-Aristotelian entelechy, Lamarck's "felt needs," Teilhard de Chardin's "principle within," but all vitalists require it.

From *Studies in the Novel* 15, no. 4 (Winter 1983). © 1983 by North Texas State University.

The man who gave Dreiser and Lewis their concept of scientific mechanism was Jacques Loeb, head of the Rockefeller Institute's Division of Experimental Biology, friend of Einstein and Rutherford, nominee many times for the Nobel Prize, and untiring warrior against vitalist doctrines. It was his "central and dominating idea" that "all living things are chemical machines." Loeb was a major hero to the intelligentsia of the 1920s, a close friend of Veblen's, admired by the usually nonadmiring Mencken, sought after by Dreiser for help in writing his most important novel, *An American Tragedy,* and the ideal scientist, Dr. Max Gottlieb, in *Arrowsmith.*

Loeb's view can be summed up in the title of a 1915 *Yale Review* essay he wrote—"Mechanistic Science and Metaphysical Romance." Matter is not brute and inert; it is in constant motion as evinced by molecules whose number in a given mass can be counted. "This puts science for a long time, and probably irrevocably, on a mechanistic basis." And since no discontinuity exists between the matter constituting living and nonliving bodies, biology must be as mechanistic as physics. It should be possible to reduce "the phenomena of instinct and consciousness" and "heredity . . . to the ultimate elements of all phenomena in nature, that is, motions of electrons, atoms or molecules." The main task for students of heredity is to determine "the chemical substances in the chromosomes which are responsible for the hereditary transmission of a quality," and "the mechanisms by which these substances give rise to the hereditary character." Such a statement, says Donald Fleming [in his introduction to Loeb's *The Mechanistic Conception of Life*], "was a plea for the discovery of DNA." In fact, Loeb anticipated DNA when he said that De Vries's theory of mutations together with Mendelian law indicates "each individual characteristic of a spirit is represented by an individual determination of the germ. This determination may be a definite chemical compound."

As a student in Germany in the 1880s, Loeb had committed himself to the famous mutual oath sworn to in 1845 by Helmholtz and three other experimental physiologists; they would account for all bodily processes in physical-chemical terms. Among their contemporaries medical materialists made declarations such as "genius is a question of phosphorous" and "the brain secretes thought the way the kidney secretes urine." Such statements recover the thinking of the *philosophes,* among whom was Cabanis who said the brain secretes thought the way the liver secretes bile.

Loeb also revived the mechanistic view of d'Holbach, Helvétius, and de la Mettrie, whose *Man, a Machine*, published anonymously in 1746, adumbrated the position Loeb set forth in *The Mechanistic Conception of Life*. American Enlightenment figures had been receptive to mechanistic materialism, especially Jefferson, who admired Cabanis. "Why may not the mode of action called thought, have been given to a material organ of peculiar structure?" Continuing, in a letter to John Adams, wherein he discourses on Cabanis's, Dugald Stuart's and Destutt Tracy's ("The ablest Metaphysicans living") investigation of "the thinking faculty of man," Jefferson states that between "Mr. Locke . . . and other materialists" and "the Spiritualists," he would, "with Mr. Locke, prefer swallowing one incomprehensibility rather than two. It requires one effort only to admit the single incomprehensibility of matter endowed with thought: and two to believe, 1st. that of an existence called Spirit, of which we have neither evidence nor idea, and then 2dly. how that spirit which has neither extension nor solidity, can put material organs into motion."

But in the reaction which followed the French Revolution, mechanism became suspect and only gradually did it again assert itself. F. W. J. Hemmings has remarked on the connection between the emergence of realism in Europe and the abandonment by advanced thinkers of a belief in transcendental values. The influence of Claude Bernard's mechanistic theories on Zola is a case in point (the other side of the coin is Dostoevsky's hatred of Bernard). Rudolph Virchow, another Helmholtz associate, who wrote an essay in 1858 entitled "The Mechanistic Concept of Life," thought the individual had the right to ask "transcendental" questions, but if he does he leaves the "public" arena of science and enters "the secret chamber of his conscience."

The pioneer positivists Loeb worked with in the public arena of science in Europe led him to his abiding convictions: physical chemistry as the key to biology, the dependence of all sciences on quantitative analysis, which may be expressed in mathematical formulae; an interest in plant and animal tropisms which enabled him to refute Darwin's argument that automatic orientation toward light was the product of a self-preservative instinct; and the production of life in the laboratory. In refuting Darwin he showed that caterpillars—"photochemical machines enslaved to the light"—starved to death if food were placed in a direction opposite from the light. Thus, with his hypothesis of photochemical substances in the head, Loeb laid the groundwork for explaining migration, spawning, and courtship ritual among birds, fish, and insects.

These findings of Loeb's, which became the basis for Dreiser's famous "chemisms," can, in the light of present knowledge, scarcely be referred to any longer as "intellectual debris" (Irving Howe's term for them), or in Lionel Trilling's version, as a special Dreiserian vagary, which must be "hustled out of sight." The human photochemical machines Dreiser created—tropistically enslaved like Clyde Griffiths to city lights, the glitter of hotel lobbies, and the effulgence of the success ethic—are very greatly attributable to Loeb's influence, an influence not, as Crick and Watson have demonstrated, to be summarily dismissed as "foolish" and "vulgar," what "the modern crowd thinks when it decides to think." Thorstein Veblen, who can scarcely be termed "one of the crowd," eagerly adopted Loebian terminology in *Absentee Ownership* and *The Instinct of Workmanship*, in which he speaks of man's "tropismatic attitudes."

Less significant as a source of metaphor was Loeb's attempt to reach the crux of biological mysticism—the process of creating life— "where so many ingenious theologians through the ages had seen their chance to slip a soul in while nobody was looking." Loeb gave the death blow to this variant of vitalism when he accomplished artificial parthenogenesis by substituting "well-known physical-chemical agents for the mysterious action of the spermatazoon." Using sodium chloride and magnesium chloride, Loeb, and the subsequent father of American genetics, T. H. Morgan, induced sea urchins to start segmentation. Ultimately larvae were brought to sexual maturity. Loeb's parthenogenetic sea urchins elicited sensational newspaper reporting and enchanted the public, calling forth from Mark Twain, another dedicated mechanist, the admonition: "Now as concerns this 'creation of life by chemical agencies.' Reader, take my advice: don't you copper it." Previously Twain had listed all those a "consensus of experts" had "coppered" (colloquial for "bets against"): Fulton, Priestly, Jenner, Pasteur, the telegraph, Atlantic cable, evolution—"all brushed into space" by "frenzied and ferocious" coalitions of medical and chemical and theological scoffers.

Many of Loeb's doctrines appear in *Arrowsmith,* which was originally to have been entitled *The Shadow of Max Gottlieb,* the name Lewis chose for Jacques Loeb. Lewis had learned about Loeb from Paul de Kruif, a young bacteriologist at the Rockefeller Institute, who had anonymously published a series of articles in *Century Magazine* on "Our Medicine Men," and who later (also anonymously) wrote the chapter on "Medicine" in *Civilization in the United States,* a compendium of the discontent of American intellectuals. De Kruif introduced

Loeb to the American public in a *Harper's* article which held that "his ideas may be of greater importance than those of Darwin." Lewis had been casting about for a heroic figure and found that his and de Kruif's ideas on the medical profession coincided. Both were a bit sentimental over the decline of the general practitioner (Lewis's grandfather, father, uncle, and older brother belonged to this vanishing breed), and both were hostile to the commercialization of the profession. But neither old- nor new-timer, they thought, comprehended the scientific method or the character of true science.

Almost at the outset Lewis, no doubt at de Kruif's prompting, raised the mechanist-vitalist question, which de Kruif saw as the heart of "true science." The "wild man" of the English department at Winnemac University, where Martin Arrowsmith is a medical student, professes himself astounded that bacteriology professor Max Gottlieb "can be blind to the vital force that creates all others." Against such "scientific sharks" who try to measure the genius of a Ben Jonson with a yardstick, he poses "[us] literary chaps with our doubtless absurd belief in beauty and loyalty and the world of dreams." The "literary playboy" is slapped down by "Encore" Edwards, head of the chemistry department, who exalts Gottlieb's "long, lonely, failure-burdened effort to synthesize antitoxin, and his diabolic pleasure in disproving his own contentions." Gottlieb himself announces "the ultimate lesson of science, which is to wait and doubt." Later when a French scientist anticipates Arrowsmith's great discovery, Gottlieb tells him: "That is science: to work and not to care—too much—if someone else gets the credit." Throughout the book Gottlieb continues to give his disciple a value system learned from Helmholtz and such heroes as "Father Koch and Father Pasteur and Brother Jacques Loeb and Brother Arrhenius."

By contrast, "Dad" Silva, Dean of the Winnemac Medical School, exemplifies R & D, or what Thomas Kuhn has called "mop-up science." His gods, Silva says, are "the men who took the discoveries of Gottlieb's gods and turned them to the use of human beings. . . . It's all very fine, this business of pure research: seeking the truth, unhampered by commercialism or fame-chasing. Getting to the bottom. Ignoring consequences and practical uses." But was this "work for a tall man at a time when heroes were building bridges, experimenting with Horseless Carriages, writing the first of the poetic Compelling Ads and selling miles of calico and cigars?" Apparently not, for Max Gottlieb had "never dined with a duchess, never received a prize, never been interviewed, never produced anything the public could understand. . . . He was, in fact, an authentic scientist."

De Kruif had begun the essay on "Medicine" in *Civilization in the United States* by asking why Americans permit the "obvious quackery" of Mary Baker Eddy and the Harvard Medical School to coexist side by side. Most Americans are gullible and the teachers, students, and alumni of medical schools are drawn from our "excessively credulous populace." Both confuse the *"art"* of medical practice with the *"science"* of the study of disease (italics, de Kruif's). Science, as Loeb was always saying, is concerned with quantitative relations of the factors governing natural phenomena. "No favourites are to be played among these factors. They are to be weighed and measured meticulously and coldly," a course of behavior impossible in a physician–patient relationship when emotions enter. The old general practitioner performed a "quasi-religious function"; his role was that of a "professional sympathizer." Such a relationship would preclude the use of laboratory "control" (a word Gottlieb is always urging on Arrowsmith). For example, says de Kruif, if a doctor wishes to test the efficacy of a serum:

> In America it is practically unknown for him to divide his cases of pneumonia into two groups of equal size, to administer his serum to Group A and to leave Group B untreated. He almost invariably has a *parti-pris* that the serum will work, and he reflects with horror that if he holds his remedy from Group B, some members of this group will die, who might otherwise have been saved. So he injects his serum into all of his patients (A and B), and if the mortality in the entire group appears to him to be lower by statistics than that observed in previous series of cases, he concludes that the value of his nostrum is proved. This is an illustration of the fallacy of the notion that medicine is a science in the modern sense.

De Kruif's example becomes the crux of *Arrowsmith*. Martin Arrowsmith discovers bacteriophage, a virus that infects bacterial cells and can be used for immunization against various diseases. An epidemic of the plague breaks out in the West Indies and Martin is dispatched there. Before he leaves he pledges to Max Gottlieb—"swore by Jacques Loeb"—that he will use a control, thus establishing the value of the immunization as completely as the method of control had established the connection between the mosquito and yellow fever. Gottlieb tells him he must pity the generations yet to come so much that you "refuse to let yourself indulge in pity for the men you will see dying." But another, less rigorous scientist—the public health crusader, Gustaf Sondelius—refuses to let himself be inoculated until Martin gets "converted to humanity," and gives the phage to everyone in St. Helena. He prophesies that Martin will eventually do so and turns out to be right, although it is not because of mass suffering. Through the worst ravages Martin steels himself, retaining a picture of Max Gottlieb's demanding eyes, and swears he will not "yield to a compassion which in the end would make all compassion futile." Even when Sondelius dies, he says, "I'm not a sentimentalist; I'm a scientist." But when Leora Arrowsmith, careless as ever, forgets to give herself an injection of phage and dies, he cries out, "Oh, damn experimentation," and distributes the phage indiscriminately.

The epidemic passes and Martin, as in de Kruif's hypothetical case, becomes a hero. He is congratulated on having established the value of bacteriophage on a large scale, and he becomes the Institute's prize exhibit. But he is uneasy about the judgment of Gottlieb, ill and bitterly disillusioned by wartime anti-German hysteria. All the way uptown to see him Martin can hear Gottlieb saying: "You were my son! I gave you eferyt'ing I knew of truth and honor, and you haf betrayed me. Get out of my sight!" But Gottlieb, sunk in senile dementia, his memory gone, speaking only German, peers uncomprehendingly at him. "Martin understood that never could he be punished now and cleansed. Gottlieb had sunk into darkness still trusting him."

Martin feels he has failed the test and later (improbably) abandons the Institute for nature's primal sanities. He sets up a laboratory to study quinine derivatives far from the Bitch Goddess of Success, cheerfully resigned to fail in the Gottliebian sense. This ending probably represents Lewis's lingering transcendentalism more than de Kruif's views. Loeb himself, although deeply disillusioned with what the war revealed about conduct, remained at the Rockefeller Institute, never believing it possible to conduct the scientific enterprise at Walden Pond.

Running through Lewis's portraits (and caricatures) of the medical profession and the health industry are tributes to Gottlieb's definition of "a clean kingdom like biology." There are frequent echoes of Jacques Loeb's insistence that "what progress humanity has made, not only in physical welfare but also in the conquest of superstition and hatred, and in the formation of a correct view of life, it owes directly or indirectly to mechanistic science." Gottlieb's program for the future is almost identical to B. F. Skinner's in his behaviorist utopia, *Walden Two*. The only real revolutionary is the authentic scientist "because he alone knowns how liddle he knows":

> He must be heartless. He lives in a cold, clean light. . . . The world has always been ruled by the Philanthropists: by the doctors that want to use therapeutic methods they do not understand, by the soldiers that want something to defend their country against. . . and see once what a fine mess of hell they haf made of the world! Maybe now it is time for the scientist, who works and searches and never goes around howling how he loves everybody!

Skinner's behavioral engineers are equally to be chosen for their allegiance to scientific principles. The majority, like de Kruif's credulous populace, is in no position to evaluate them nor is it patient enough to maintain the cold, unbiased harness of a scientific experiment. If this is despotism, says Skinner, better the despotism of scientific intelligence than the despotism of the charlatans, demagogues, salesmen, and educators who have so far dominated the world.

Loeb himself answered the question which vitalists always ask. If men are only chemical mechanisms, how can there be an ethics for them? The answer is that instincts are at the root of ethics and are as hereditary as body structure. We eat because, "machine-like," we are compelled to do so. But we are also compelled by "the sexual instincts with its poetry and its chain of consequences, the maternal instincts with the felicity and the suffering caused by them, the instinct of workmanship" (which he shared with or bestowed upon Veblen). Loeb also postulates an instinct central to the Enlightenment's faculty of sociability. "We seek and enjoy the fellowship of human beings because hereditary conditions compel us to do so. We struggle for justice and truth since we are instinctively compelled to see our fellow beings happy." Jefferson's version was in answer to why good acts give us pleasure: "Because nature hath implanted in our breasts a love of others, a sense of duty to them, a moral instinct, in short, which prompts us irresistibly to feel and to succor their distresses."

II

Dreiser came to Loeb somewhat differently. He had learned about him from Mencken, and what he learned reinforced his reliance on

Herbert Spencer, who had stated in *First Principles* that "life in its simplest form is the correspondence of certain inner physico-chemical actions with certain other physico-chemical actions." Dreiser, an autodidact, kept returning in the course of his education to mechanists such as Elmer Gates, Carl Snyder, and George Crile. Gates, an amateur physiologist who built himself a Wundt-like laboratory out of the proceeds of such typically American inventions as a diamagnetic gold separator, an electric loom, and a septic brewing technique, wrote a book on the chemical nature of thought, which he lent to Dreiser in manuscript. Gates's constructs were fairly fanciful, but he gave Dreiser some images to use in *Sister Carrie.* Gates maintained that the metabolism of brain cells paralleled the biochemical laws of body metabolism. Noble thoughts produce nourishing chemical changes which, in effect, stimulate the creation of "more mind." Depressing emotions produce poisonous chemical changes. Not yet knowing Loeb and therefore unable to use tropismatic imagery, although he moves toward it when Hurstwood dies in the snow looking at Carrie's name on the marquee in "incandescent fire," Dreiser describes the atmosphere of New York after Chicago as "like a chemical reagent. One day of it, like one drop of the other, will so affect and discolor the views, the aims, the desires of the mind, that it will thereafter remain forever dyed." Later, as Hurstwood's fortunes decline, Dreiser, duplicating Gates's terminology almost exactly, writes: "Now it has been shown experimentally that a constantly subdued frame of mind produces certain poisons in the blood, called kastastates, just as virtuous feelings of pleasure and delight produce helpful chemicals, called anastates. The poisons, generated by remorse, inveigh against the system and eventually produce marked physical deterioration. To this Hurstwood was subject."

Carl Snyder, an editorial writer for the *Washington Post* and Loeb's foremost popularizer, stated flatly in presenting the Loebian view, "the mysterious vital force . . . does not exist." It is now clear that "the line demarking the domains of organic and mineral chemism is a figment of the mind." George Crile, a Cleveland surgeon, was the third apostle of Loeb's. In *Man, an Adaptive Mechanism,* he warned against allowing the vocabulary of vitalism to invade scientific thought through such teleological terms as "innate faculty" or "will" or "desire to live." Crile then went on to describe the mechanisms of bodily adaptation. The body is operated by electric power and it fabricates mechanisms for the production and storage of energy.

Before starting to work on *An American Tragedy,* Dreiser sought an introduction to Loeb, began writing him, and visited his laboratory at Woods Hole, a marine biology station (Dreiser had always been interested in ocean life, as the well-known parables of the lobster and squid and Black Grouper demonstrate, but he also used the shark and the blue fish, the whale and minnow, as giant and pygmy symbols for American class structure). At about the time he met Loeb he took out a reading room in the New York Public Library to do serious study in physics and chemistry.

Reading Loeb, Dreiser became fascinated with "those rearranging chemisms upon which all the morality or immorality of the world is based." It was those chemisms as they rearranged themselves in Clyde Griffith's consciousness which became the crux of the novel. Earlier in *Jennie Gerhardt,* Dreiser had referred generally to "the chemistry of life" or "chemical physical attraction," and Frank Cowperwood's behavior is the product of "some mulch of chemistry," but his decision to use "chemism" apparently came from his absorption in Loeb and his acquaintance with the work of Freud. Loeb himself never used the word "chemism," except in public speaking when he sometimes lapsed into Germanisms, and the term has been excised out of Freud's British translations and replaced by the more innocuous "chemistry." "Chemism" is a word with an uncertain history, originating with Hegel. Dreiser apparently picked it up from A. A. Brill, Freud's American translator and mentor to a generation of Greenwich Village intellectuals. He and Dreiser became friends while Dreiser was writing and visiting Loeb. *An American Tragedy,* therefore, represents a confluence of two views—Freud's and Loeb's. Simultaneously Dreiser was converted to socialism. Thus Clyde's "rearranging chemisms" were shaped by that society Mencken described so cruelly and Clyde longed for so desperately: that "bugaboo" aristocracy which is thoroughly "bogus," and made up of harsh and terrible taboos. "One gets into it only onerously, but out of it very easily." To get in the applicant must show a talent for abasement. It would ruin him "to drink coffee from his saucer, or to marry a chambermaid with a gold tooth"—poor Roberta—or "join the Seventh Day Adventists" or "wear celluloid collars" or even set up a plea for ordinary decency. In fact, James T. Farrell feels Dreiser's social determinism was more important than his "biologicism."

The "biologicism" was a somewhat uncertain blend of Freud and Loeb. Loeb himself thought the mechanistic approach should be applied to psychiatry, and his own inclinations were toward Pavlov.

Like Loeb, Freud was a product of the Helmholtzian tradition (using Helmholtzian hydraulic metaphors to a great extent), and he considered himself a mechanist. Moreover, he continually revised his work to incorporate new biochemical findings. He esteemed Loeb greatly, he wrote him, for the "boldness of your intentions and the beauty of your results," and wished he would not "reject the strange path on which I try to come close to the riddles of life." But Loeb did not return the compliment. He felt Freudianism, like Charcot's hysteria "a la mode," was a passing fashion based on inexact methods.

William Phillips has pointed out that the prevailing imagery of *An American Tragedy* is not chemic, but made up of dreams and witchery. Nevertheless, the word occurs in the most crucial section of the book: the much-debated passage wherein Clyde's responsibility for Roberta's death is brought into question. At the cataclysmic moment, Clyde is overcome by "a sudden palsy of the will—of courage—of hate or rage sufficient. . .a *chemic* revulsion against death or murderous brutality . . .a static between a painful compulsion to do and yet not to do" (italics mine). In an almost classic instance of William James's theory of the emotions, his pupils dilate, his body tenses and contracts. Roberta, noting his strange appearance, rises in the boat and crawls along the keel, projecting the motherly solicitation Clyde both clings to and despises. He senses "the profoundness of his own failure, his own cowardice or inadequateness," and feels "a submerged hate" both for himself and Roberta. She draws near, tries to take his hand, and he flings out, "but not even then with any intention to do other than free himself of her—her touch—her pleading-consoling sympathy—her presence forever—God!" Rising, Roberta seeks to take his hand in hers and the camera, which Clyde is unconsciously holding tight, pushes against her and throws her back sideways. The stimulus of her sharp scream, the lurch of the boat, and the cuts on her nose and lip trigger further responses. He rises "half to assist or recapture her and half to apologize for the unintended blow," and in doing so capsizes the boat. Thereafter Clyde debates with himself and his Efrit (a genie or inner voice which has been urging Roberta's death on him) over his responsibility for not rescuing her, knowing she cannot swim, but the crucial scene itself was rendered in mechanistic stimulus-response and reflex arc terms.

Dreiser was an inconsistent mechanist, as Eliseo Vivas claims, and off and on he came close to embracing what Loeb felt was the most insidious form vitalist doctrines took—the attempt to transform the law of persistence of force or energy into some sort of Emersonian immanence doctrine. The mind, operating everywhere through particles of electrical energy, was frequently seen to resemble the Oversoul, particularly when transmitted by Darwinian popularizers like John Fiske. Fiske found immanence "a particularly attractive way" of fusing the older Emersonian doctrine with the new evolutionary creed. Loeb's adversary, Wilhelm Ostwald, who finally had to admit molecules existed, had created a new development of energetics, Loeb charged, substituting an "energetical imperative" for the categorical imperative. Dreiser was responding to such an "energetical imperative" when he wrote in 1934 that "I can find nothing that is not mind." As he grew older he came increasingly to contend that "the nature of God, or the creative force that appears to operate directly through matter-energy as well as the laws and spatial conditions environing the same is, in fact, the one reality—universal creative reality." He started identifying the "Supreme Directive Force" with "Spirit, Brahma, Divine Essence, or Force." According to two of his biographers [Robert Elias and Marguerite Tjader], he underwent two mystical experiences which confirmed him in a transcendental view of nature. Once he spoke to a puff adder and thought the snake understood him. Another time, coming out of the Carnegie Biological Laboratory, he saw evidence of a yellow flower of the same design and detail he had just been examining under a microscope. Suddenly—just as if he were a twentieth-century Paley— it became clear "there must be a divine, creative Intelligence behind all this—Not just a blind force."

One must be careful about this evidence, based on what he is supposed to have stated to two biographers anxious to refute Dreiser-as-Mechanist. John Berryman calls the Elias biography "reprehensible." But Dreiser's behavior in his last few years was nothing if not syncretistically quixotic: almost simultaneously he joined the Communist Party, embraced Quakerism and Buddhism, and took communion on Good Friday.

Nevertheless, through it all he kept at work on what he expected to be his magnum opus, a work entitled *The Mechanism Called Man,* for which he had accumulated forty-seven boxes of notes. Some of the chapter headings run: Mechanism called the Universe; Mechanism called Life; The Mechanism called Man; Mechanism called Mind; Mechanism called Memory. His definitive words on the subject of Jacques Loeb indicate, as Ellen Moers points out, that he never abandoned his Loebian views: "The more I examined the various scientific attempts at an interpretation of life . . . the more I respect and admire Loeb. He has not been superseded—he has not even as yet been approximated."

Jacques Loeb, the idealized scientist, seems to have been Lewis's and Dreiser's primary culture hero and the catalyst for their two outstanding works.

III

Sir Francis Crick says that "exact knowledge is the enemy of vitalism." But although we know the "automatic" mechanism by which our present biological complexity evolved from simple chemical compounds—natural selection, which requires no special "life force" or directing "intelligence"—and we also know the copying mechanisms which can replicate genetic information, nonetheless, there has been a "resurgence" of vitalist doctrines. They are especially fashionable in literary circles and Crick cites the popularity of Teilhard de Chardin and Michael Polanyi. Sir P. B. Medawar in a presidential address to the British Association of Scientists makes the same complaint. Among intelligent and learned men, an "elevated kind of barminess" is resorted to, comparable to the mystical synthesis between science and religion created by seventeenth-century Cambridge Platonists—the cult of de Chardin, and "a revival of faith in the Wisdom of the East."

Crick attributed the resurgence of vitalism to the intrinsic difficulties of comprehending exactly what happened with the original proteins and nucleic acid three or four thousand million years ago. Isaac Asimov cites befuddlement at how the 2,400,000,000,000,000,000 permutations and combinations in the polypeptide chain of twenty amino acids can possibly replicate genetic information. We also still have reservations about the borderline between the living and nonliving, Crick says. We therefore prefer to heroize consciousness rather than explain "*all* biology in terms of physics and chemistry," as Loeb had prophesied we would.

Medawar, on the other hand, sees the trend toward vitalism as a failure of nerve stemming from our prevailing sense of decay and especially our fear of the "deteriorization" of the world through technological innovation. Consequently, "a kind of Jacobean melancholy" has set in, again especially among literary men. Medawar is also critical of writers who make their texts hard to follow by means of "digressions, paradoxes, impressive sounding references to Gödel, Wittgenstein, and topology, 'in' jokes, trollopy metaphors." Writers have always used scientific metaphors. It is a massive confusion of realms, however, to apply the constructs of astronomy to government (the macrocosm-microcosm concept) or of biology to economics (Spencer's survival of the fittest). Recently the trend has accelerated with quantum jumps, vectors, Brownian motion, entropy, indeterminacy being applied indiscriminately to educational, social, political, economic, and psychological areas. It has been said that if the indeterminacy principle had been christened "the principle of limited measureability," it would never have been applied on such a wholesale scale. But indeterminacy has such a splendidly metaphysical sound.

As P. W. Bridgman predicted many years ago, the principle, applicable only to fine-scale phenomena, where the scientist, "whenever he penetrates to the atomic or electronic level in his analysis, he finds things acting in a way for which he can assign no cause," would be chiefly influential on "the man in the street." True only of the "infinitesimal world," it will "let loose a veritable intellectual spree of licentious and debauched thinking." Refusing to limit the statement to the electron, the "man in the street will, therefore, twist the statement . . . that the scientist has penetrated as far as he can with the tools at his command" into an "imagined beyond," which will "become the playground of the imagination of every mystic and dreamer." Such a domain will be made the basis of an orgy of rationalizing, of "the soul," of "vital process," a "solution of the age-long problem of the freedom of the will." "God will lurk in the shadows," while at the same time, "the atheist will find the justification of his contention that chance rules the universe."

Despite Bridgman's warning, philosophers, sociologists, historians, novelists have applied the principle indiscriminately. Thus David Riesman could say of political power that it is "situational and mercurial; it resists attempts to locate it the way a molecule, under the Heisenberg principle, resists attempts simultaneously to locate it and time its velocity." R. P. Blackmur could wrongheadedly blame the physicists for destroying "the last healthy remnants of moral determinism" and creating the "malicious criticism of knowledge."

Various contemporary writers are guilty of the same name-and concept-dropping Medawar complains about (it is hard to think of a current novel that does not cite "the world is all the case there is"). Pynchon uses the Heisenberg principle to explain the difference between listening to and telling sea stories and the relationship between analgesics and drug addiction. The vitalism Loeb and Crick battle remains a constant in literary discourse, usually in the form of mechanistic behavior-ism—a bête noire for many for whom the left brain seems to stand in need of instant lobotomy. But in *Love in the Ruins,* Walker Percy has actually recreated Max Gottlieb.

In Percy's novel, subtitled *Adventures of a Bad Catholic at a Time Near the End of the World,* Max Gottlieb appears as a kindly neo-behavorist, best friend to Tom More, a shaky, middle-aged psychia-trist in the latter days of the United States. (This is a variant from a norm where most behaviorists seem to resemble Pynchon's ultimate conditioner, castrator Pavlovian Ned Pointsman, who starts to crack up when he begins to suspect cause does not always produce effect.)

In Percy's futurama, the wars between San Francisco and Los Angeles, Chicago and Cicero are over; wolves have been seen in Cleveland. In Paradise Parish, Louisiana, Percy's Yoknapatawpha County, Bantus and Knotheads are still fighting, motels and shopping centers have reverted to water moccasins, screech owls, and raccoons. Yet in the midst of the wasteland, behavioral engineering, sex clinics, geriatric rehabilitation, communes, a heavy sodium chloride project underneath the Sugar Bowl, baton twirlers, defrocked priests who run the Vaginal Computer at the Love Clinic, and backyard barbecues still flourish. "The center did not hold. However, the Gross National Product continues to rise." Percy, who fancies himself a black humor-ist, brings in the now obligatory array of characters: ex-Ayn Randers, Choctaw Zionists, ESPers, UFOers, deserters from the Swedish Army, and graduates of Bob Jones University.

More, the Bad Catholic, has a great new invention, a Lapsometer (something like Emerson's Realometer for measuring man's capacities). But the Lapsometer measures man's fall into sin. More important, through adding an ionizer and focusing on the pineal gland, it stands to become "the stethoscope of the spirit." "Suppose," says More, like his famous progenitor, "I could hit on the right dosage and weld the broken self whole! What if man could reenter paradise?" Patients suffering from "angelism-bestialism" might be cured. Thus More's Qualitative-Quantitative Ontological Lapsometer (MOQUOL) joins a similar array of machines: Barth's UNIVAC and Pynchon's SHROUD and SHOCK.

Percy's game becomes clear. Under the guise of satire, he is argu-ing for original sin and vitalism. One of his colleagues, a polylingual black, does not go along with his ideas of "measuring and treating the deep perturbations of the soul." "Unfortunately, there still persists in the medical profession," Percy authorially comments, "the quaint superstition that only that which is visible is real. Thus the soul is not real." At this point Percy delivers his body blow. "Then, friend, how come you are shaking?" More has created "the first caliper of the soul and the first hope of bridging the dread chasm that has rent the soul of Western man ever since the famous philosopher Descartes ripped body loose from mind and turned the very soul into a ghost that haunts its own house."

As expected, Max Gottlieb, who once sewed up Tom More's wrists, delivers the mechanist argument. But Gottlieb is no caricature. Instead he is "a prodigy," "a young prince . . . young Jesus confounding his elders."

> Here's an oddity. Max the unbeliever, a lapsed Jew, believes in the orderliness of creation, acts on with energy and charity. I the believer, having swallowed the whole Thing, God Jews Christ Church, find the world a madhouse and a madhouse home. Max the atheist sees things like Saint Thomas Aquinas, ranged, orderly, connected up.

Yet Max seems oddly old-fashioned. He had tamed Tom More's suicidal terror by naming it; later he suggests a Skinner box to condition away his contradictions. (Tom insists on feeling guilty so he can undergo the sacrament of penance.) Gottlieb does not believe in guilt. "But if I never felt guilt," Tom says, "I'd really be up the creek." Poor Max does his best in a curiously dated way, but he cannot really see big sin. "Like Freud himself, he is both Victorian and anatomical, speaking one moment delicately of 'paying court to the ladies' . . . and the next of genitalia and ejaculations."

In fact, he probably could not see a great deal of what Percy sees—the goodness, for instance in Leroy Ledbetter's soul which started a riot five years earlier when he refused to let a bushy-haired Bantu couple from Tougaloo College have an alley in his bowling lanes.

> Where did the terror come from. Not from the violence. . . . Not from Leroy's wrongness. . . . No, it came from Leroy's goodness, that he is a decent, sweet-natured man who would help you if you needed help, go out of the way and bind up a stranger's wounds. No, the terror comes from the goodness and what lies beneath, some fault in the soul's terrain so deep that all is well on top, evil grins like good, but something shears and tears deep down and the very ground stirs beneath one's feet.

This is apparently what the metaphysical vision consists of—the mystery of iniquity. And the metaphysical cure is in "the new Christ, the spotted Christ, the maculate Christ." The methods of the old Christ did not work. "The new Christ lies drunk in a ditch." Tom and Leroy pick him up and carry him off. "They love the new Christ and so they love each other." But Percy is too *au courant* to leave it all that simple. A super government agent (higher than CIA) who speaks behaviorese—"we facilitate social interaction in order to isolate factors" —steals the lapsometers and screws up the angelism dosage for purposes of demonstration. The result, according to More, would render a subject "totally abstracted from himself, totally alienated from the concrete world." High-level angelism would leave him prey to the first abstract notion proposed, and he would "kill anybody who gets in his way, torture, execute, wipe out entire populations all with the best possible motives and the best possible intention, in fact in the name of peace and freedom, etcetera."

The novel ends with More living with one wife—under the inspiration of Abraham he had considered three—in Paradise, now gone ninety-nine percent Bantu. How? They had struck oil and now Bantu golfers are wearing rediscovered knickerbockers and earmuffs and delivering Christmas baskets to disadvantaged peckerwood children. Tom does public penance, which John XXIV has reinstated, and goes home to barbecue in the backyard and contemplate the new coalition: "Kennedy, Evers, Goldberg, Stevenson, L. Q. C. Lamar." So much for Jacques Loeb's and B. F. Skinner's version of the future.

If Percy is to be considered representative, the literary psychology still answers to Santayana's definition. No wonder, then, that Dreiser and Lewis never seem to attain a permanent resuscitation.

Sinclair Lewis, Max Gottlieb, and Sherlock Holmes

Robert L. Coard

The character of Max Gottlieb, the pure scientist of Sinclair Lewis's best seller *Arrowsmith* (1925) and the inspirer of its protagonist Martin Arrowsmith, is, in the words of Paul de Kruif, Lewis's scientific collaborator on *Arrowsmith,* "a muddy mélange of my revered chief, Professor Novy, and of Jacques Loeb, who was my master in a philosophy of the mechanistic conception of life." Paul de Kruif is correct in identifying two parts of the "muddy mélange": Jacques Loeb (1859–1924), the German-American physiologist, famous for his work with tropisms and artificial parthenogenesis, and de Kruif's colleague for two years at the Rockefeller Institute; and Frederick Novy (1864–1957), professor and chairman of the Department of Bacteriology at the University of Michigan for many years and de Kruif's much-admired teacher. Perhaps the murkiness of the mélange that went into the formation of the character of Lewis's scientific genius Max Gottlieb prevented de Kruif from identifying a third element in Lewis's creation: Arthur Conan Doyle's renowned detective, Sherlock Holmes.

Sinclair Lewis makes the comparison between Max Gottlieb and Sherlock Holmes in the thirteenth chapter of *Arrowsmith:* "However abstracted and impractical, Gottlieb would have made an excellent Sherlock Holmes—if anybody who would have made an excellent Sherlock Holmes would have been willing to be a detective. His mind burned through appearances to actuality."

From *Modern Fiction Studies* 31, no. 3 (Autumn 1985). © 1985 by Purdue Research Foundation, West Lafayette, Indiana.

Perhaps even more convincing to show the relationship between Doyle's Sherlock Holmes and Lewis's Max Gottlieb is their shared hawk imagery, suggesting keenness and strength of spirit. Sherlock Holmes's "thin, hawk-like nose" ("A Study in Scarlet") and "his hawk-like nose" thrust into the matter of "The Red-Headed League" reappear in Gottlieb's "jut of his hawk nose" and "his hawk nose bony" in *Arrowsmith*. Again Holmes's "clear-cut, hawk-like features" in "The Sign of the Four" remind one of Gottlieb's "hawk eyes." Lewis even carries the hawk image from face to fingers, supplying Gottlieb with "talon fingers."

Thinness, tallness, and asceticism are other characteristics that Lewis appropriated for his scientist from Doyle's detective. Holmes's "tall, lean figure" in "The Valley of Fear" could readily be mistaken for Gottlieb's "lean, tall figure" in *Arrowsmith*. Similarly, Holmes's "thin hands" in the same story match the scientist's "thin hands" in Lewis's novel. In lengthier quotations from each source, the reader will notice not only a mutual thinness but asceticism and the power of abstraction. In "The Valley of Fear" Watson describes how Holmes's "thin, eager features became more attenuated with the asceticism of complete mental concentration"; Lewis depicts Gottlieb emerging from his University of Winnemac laboratory at midnight: "a tall figure, ascetic, self-contained, apart. His swart cheeks were gaunt, his nose high-bridged and thin. . . . He was unconscious of the world."

Both men are nervous pacers. Gottlieb "pacing the floor, his long arms fantastically knotted behind his thin back," is close to Holmes as he "paced about the room in uncontrollable agitation, with a flush upon his sallow cheeks, and a nervous clasping and unclasping of his long thin hands" in "The Five Orange Pips." And Holmes's "long, thin back curved over a chemical vessel" in "The Adventure of the Dancing Men" would fit readily into Gottlieb's laboratory. Indeed, Gottlieb taking "a hypodermic needle from the instrument-bath" and exerting "a quick down thrust of the hypodermic needle" on a guinea pig is not all that different in technique from Holmes punching his arm with a hypodermic needle for his cocaine injection. With Sherlock Holmes as one of his progenitors, it's no wonder that Max Gottlieb made this suggestion to Martin Arrowsmith if he should have trouble with a research problem: "When you get stuck in a problem, I have a fine collection of detective stories in my office."

Paul de Kruif's *Sweeping Wind* shows that the Lewis references to Sherlock Holmes are not casual ones. At one stage in the creation of

Arrowsmith, Lewis switched his proposed collaboration with de Kruif from a novel to a series of short stories having a kind of public health detective for hero: "We were going to do a series of short stories, not a novel; stories with a new type of hero, a character—bacteriologist, doctor, public health detective—all in one." Norman Hapgood, then editor of *Hearst's International Magazine* and formerly editor of *Collier's Weekly* during its 1903 resurrection of Holmes, was interested in Lewis's idea "for a magazine serial, introducing a new fiction character that Red was sure might rival Sherlock Holmes."

Though the idea of making the hero of such a series a "public health detective" was new, Lewis's idea for a series built around a central investigative figure went back at least to 1910 when he proposed such a series to Jack London about the World Police to be unified by a central character, the Man of the World Police. The Lewis proposal, which he hoped to sell to Jack London, is filled with references to Sherlock Holmes: "I've been for years watching out for series. That's where Conan Doyle made his stake—starting the Sherlock Holmes Series; a bunch of stories which, each singly, would be lost; but which unified by the central figure of Sherlock Holmes, made Conan Doyle all he is today." Lewis advised London to master everything about the Man of the World Police "from his ideas on matrimony up to his brand of tobacco" and added, "He need not—should not, and, with you writing, would not—be in the least like Sherlock Holmes, but Holmes offers suggestions, nevertheless."

Elsewhere Lewis expanded on the value of the human interest detail in characterization, again citing Sherlock Holmes: "Mr. Sherlock Holmes remains our favorite detective . . . because we behold him, smoking his pipe, morosely fiddling, loafing in his dressing-gown." Considering the preceding, it might not be too fantastic to suggest that Max Gottlieb's wife with "her warming of his old-fashioned nightgown" handles a garment manufactured in the same factory as Sherlock Holmes's dressing-gown.

Besides employing picturesque detail to characterize, Lewis also liked using startling character contrast, and that too is detective story technique. The master brain usually finds himself surrounded by dolts. In "A Study in Scarlet," for example, Holmes contrasts with the obtuse men of Scotland Yard, Lestrade and Gregson, unimaginative, publicity-seeking bureaucrats, not at all unlike such nincompoops as Dr. Rippleton Holabird and Dr. A. De Witt Tubbs, who trod the corridors of the McGurk Institute along with true scientists Max

Gottlieb and his spiritual son, Martin Arrowsmith. Significantly, Arrowsmith is also compared to a detective: "A detective, hunting the murderer of bacteria, he stood with his head back, scratching his chin, scratching his memory for like cases of microörganisms committing suicide or being slain without perceptible cause." As Arrowsmith races to the library to consult authorities, one seems to see Holmes consulting equivalent cases in his exhaustive files.

Though the subject matter differs, the rapid narrative pace, the startling surprises, and quick climaxes of the Sherlock Holmes adventures are repeated in *Arrowsmith*. Things happen. Consider the ninth chapter. Arrowsmith dines with Clif Clawson and Babbitt, quarrels with Gottlieb, is suspended from medical school, borrows money from Clif, goes on the bum, works at miscellaneous jobs, travels west, visits his girlfriend in North Dakota, suffers her family, elopes, reaches a rough compromise with his wife's relatives, heads back to medical school alone.

For the reader still unconvinced of the presence of Sherlock Holmes in *Arrowsmith,* another explicit reference to Holmes in the same novel may be cited. Clif Clawson, Arrowsmith's boardinghouse roommate at medical school, is depicted as "sitting on the small of his back, shoeless feet upon the study table, reading a Sherlock Holmes story which rested on the powerful volume of Osler's Medicine which he considered himself to be reading." The reference here to Sherlock Holmes is deprecating, but Lewis was often ambivalent about fellow popular writers like Doyle and Kipling, as though he were ashamed of his fondness for them. He supplies the repulsive Elmer Gantry, for example, with Doyle books for his meager rooming-house bookshelf at Terwillinger College: "Elmer owned two volumes of Conan Doyle, one of E. P. Roe, and a priceless copy of 'Only a Boy.' " On the other hand, an admirable character, Neil Kingsblood, of the late Lewis novel *Kingsblood Royal,* also possesses Doyle volumes: "And here were his own not-very-numerous books. The set of Kipling, the set of O. Henry, the set of Sherlock Holmes."

The references to Doyle and Sherlock Holmes in Lewis's fiction and nonfiction are more often favorable than disparaging and convince the reader that Doyle was something of a factor in shaping Lewis's literary style and substance. In the novel *The Trail of the Hawk,* published a decade before *Arrowsmith,* Lewis has an autobiographical character, Carl Ericson, a Minnesota boy living in the small town of Joralemon, discover Holmes with emotions approaching ecstasy: "Carl met Sherlock Holmes in a paper-bound book, during a wait for flocks of mallards on the duck-pass. . . . He crouched down . . . gun across knees, and read for an hour without moving. As he tramped home. . . he kept his gun cocked and under his elbow, ready for the royal robber who was dogging the personage of Baker Street." This reaction does not differ essentially from that expressed in a 1943 estimate of the character Bazarov in a preface Lewis wrote for Ivan Turgenev's *Fathers and Sons:* "His name is one of the few in fiction that lives on, like Quixote and Micawber and Sherlock Holmes, more immortal than all but a few actual personages."

Using de Kruif's recollections of Loeb for Max Gottlieb's Jewish background, German accent, and mechanistic philosophy and de Kruif's recollections of Novy at the University of Michigan for the University of Winnemac passages, Lewis still felt it necessary to appropriate the hawk face, nervous pacings, thin, tall asceticism, and power of abstraction from Sherlock Holmes to animate his scientist. Though with different subject matter, Lewis employed the graphic descriptive detail, the dramatic contrast of characters, and the thundering surprises and climaxes of the Sherlock Holmes adventures in his novel. Lacking background in science, Lewis wanted to understand Gottlieb imaginatively, and to do so he drew on Sherlock Holmes the brilliant chemist, the role in which Watson first glimpsed the master detective in "A Study in Scarlet," as he worked alone in the chemical laboratory of a London hospital in "a lofty chamber" with tables "which bristled with retorts, test-tubes, and little Bunsen lamps with their blue flickering flames." Lewis's scientist Max Gottlieb, the Jewish genius married to an unintellectual bourgeois Catholic wife, the father of the faithful Miriam and the wastrel Robert, is, too obviously, a character constructed for striking contrast and not for psychological consistency. Lewis, it would appear, added the Sherlock Holmes elements to the Gottlieb mélange to increase vividness, but in the 1980s when the research scientist is no longer a novelty in fiction, it seems Lewis is laboring unduly for effect.

Calling attention to the role of Sherlock Holmes in Lewis's creation of Gottlieb does remind the student of Lewis of the need to pay attention to Lewis's sources in other popular literature as well as in biography, contemporary events, and the contributions of research assistants. Lewis was a popular writer who succeeded by carefully studying other popular writers and absorbing their practices. Finally, Holmes-like, one might reason from the detective story fragments scattered throughout *Arrowsmith* that its author wanted to write a detective story. And so he did. Though Lewis never got his wish, in a letter to his publisher Alfred Harcourt dated December 27, 1923, composed while Lewis was furiously at work on the *Arrowsmith* manuscript, he contemplated his next project: "It'll be, I think, either a lovely detective story I've enjoyed planning, or the big religious novel I've planned so long."

Chronology

1885	Harry Sinclair Lewis born February 7 at Sauk Centre, Minnesota, second son of Edwin J. Lewis and Emma Kermott Lewis.
1890–92	Attends public schools in Sauk Centre.
1891	Mother dies.
1892	Father marries Isabel Warnper.
1901–3	Writes and works as a typesetter for Sauk Centre *Herald* and Sauk Centre *Avalanche.* Attends school at Oberlin Academy in preparation for Yale.
1903–6	Attends Yale. Writes for Yale *Literary Magazine* and *Courant;* edits *Literary Magazine.* Travels to England during the summers of 1904 and 1906. Returns to Sauk Centre in 1905 and plans the novel *The Village Virus.*
1906	Leaves Yale. Lives on Upton Sinclair's utopian farm in Englewood, New Jersey.
1906–7	Lives in New York. Works at temporary jobs, including editorial work and free-lance writing for magazines. Travels to Panama in 1907 to work on canal.
1907–8	Returns to Yale and receives degree in June 1908.
1912–14	Publishes *Hike and the Aeroplane* under the pseudonym "Tom Graham." Marries Grace Livingstone Hegger in April 1914 in New York. Publishes *Our Mr. Wrenn.*
1915	Resigns position with George H. Doran Company after the publication of *The Trail of the Hawk* to become full-time writer.
1917	Publishes *The Job* and *The Innocents.* Son Wells born.
1919	Publishes *Free Air.* His play *Hobohemia* produced in New York.

1920	*Main Street* published.
1921–22	Begins to lecture. Travels to Europe to write *Babbitt,* which is published in 1922.
1923	Travels with Paul de Kruif collecting material to write *Arrowsmith.* Writes *Arrowsmith* in France, revises it in London.
1924–25	Returns to the United States. Publishes *Arrowsmith.*
1926	Publishes *Mantrap.* Researches *Elmer Gantry.* Refuses Pulitzer Prize. Father dies.
1927	*Elmer Gantry* published. Returns to Europe and completes *The Man Who Knew Coolidge.*
1928	Publishes *The Man Who Knew Coolidge.* Divorces wife and marries Dorothy Thompson one month later. Returns to the U.S. and finishes *Dodsworth.*
1929	*Dodsworth* published.
1930	Second son born. Lewis awarded Nobel Prize.
1933	*Ann Vickers* published.
1934	Publishes *Work of Art* and assists in the dramatization of *Dodsworth. Jayhawker,* a play, produced in New York.
1935	Publishes *Selected Short Stories* and *It Can't Happen Here.* Elected to membership in the National Institute of Arts and Letters.
1936	Yale confers an honorary degree on Lewis. The Federal Theater Project produces *It Can't Happen Here.*
1938	Publishes *The Prodigal Parents* and contributes weekly book columns for *Newsweek.* Acts in lead role of touring production of *Angela Is Twenty-Two.*
1940	Publishes *Bethel Merriday* and teaches writing class at the University of Wisconsin.
1942–43	Divorces second wife. Publishes *Gideon Planish.*
1944–45	Son Wells killed in Alsace. Publishes *Cass Timberlane* and contributes monthly book reviews to *Esquire.*
1947	*Kingsblood Royal* published.
1949	Publishes *The God-Seeker* and sails for Italy.
1951	Dies in Rome on January 10 of heart disease. Ashes returned to Sauk Centre. *World So Wide* published posthumously.

Contributors

HAROLD BLOOM, Sterling Professor of the Humanities at Yale University, is the author of *The Anxiety of Influence, Poetry and Repression,* and many other volumes of literary criticism. His forthcoming study, *Freud: Transference and Authority,* attempts a full-scale reading of all of Freud's major writings. A MacArthur Prize Fellow, he is general editor of five series of literary criticism published by Chelsea House. During 1987-88, he served as Charles Eliot Norton Professor of Poetry at Harvard University.

FREDERIC I. CARPENTER is a research associate in English at the University of California, Berkeley. He recently edited *The Arte and Crafte of Rhetorycke* by Leonard Lox.

CHARLES E. ROSENBERG is Professor of History at the University of Pennsylvania. He is the author of *The Cholera Years: The U.S. in 1832, 1849, and 1866* and *The Trial of Assassin Guiteau,* as well as the editor of *Healing and History.* He has also published essays on the history of American science and American social and intellectual history.

MARILYN MORGAN HELLEBERG has recently published *Beyond T. M. A.: A Practical Guide to the Lost Tradition of Christian Meditation* and *A Guide to Christian Meditation.*

LYON N. RICHARDSON has been Professor of English and Director of University Libraries at Western Reserve University. He has also been an editor of *The Heritage of American Literature* and is the author of *History of Early American Magazines.*

MARTIN LIGHT is Professor of English at Purdue University and has co-authored *Critical Approaches to American Literature* and *The World of Words: A Language Reader.* He has also edited *Studies in* Babbitt and has written essays on Hemingway and Lewis.

MARY G. LAND is Professor of English at Washington State University.

ROBERT L. COARD is Professor of English at St. Cloud State University in Minnesota and has published several articles on Sinclair Lewis.

Bibliography

Anderson, David, ed. *MidAmerica III*. East Lansing: Michigan State University, Midwestern Press, 1977.

———. *MidAmerica IV*. East Lansing: Michigan State University, Midwestern Press, 1977.

Austin, Allen. "An Interview with Sinclair Lewis." *University of Kansas City Review* 24 (1958): 199–210.

Babcock, C. Merton. "Americanisms in the Novels of Sinclair Lewis." *American Speech* 35 (May 1960): 110–16.

Baden, A. L., ed. *To the Young Writer*. Ann Arbor: University of Michigan Press, 1965.

Beck, Warren. "How Good Is Sinclair Lewis?" *College English* 9 (1948): 77–80.

Bloomfield, Morton W., ed. *The Interpretation of Narrative: Theory and Practice*. Harvard English Studies, no. 1. Cambridge: Harvard University Press, 1970.

Bode, Carl, ed. *The Young Rebel in American Literature*. London: Heinemann, 1959.

Bradbury, Malcolm, and David Palmer, eds. *The American Novel and the Nineteen Twenties*. Stratford-upon-Avon Studies, no. 13. London: E. Arnold, 1971.

Brieger, Gert H. *"Arrowsmith* and the History of Medicine in America." *Mobius* 2 (July 1982): 23–38.

Brown, Daniel R. "Lewis's Satire—A Negative Emphasis." *Renascence* 18, no. 2 (1966): 63–72.

Bucco, Martin. "The Serialized Novels of Sinclair Lewis." *Western American Literature* 4 (1969): 416–23.

Coard, Robert L. "Names in the Fiction of Sinclair Lewis." *The Georgia Review* 16 (1962): 318–29.

Cohen, Hennig, ed. *Landmarks of American Writing*. New York: Basic Books, 1969.

Conroy, Stephen S. "Sinclair Lewis's Sociological Imagination." *American Literature* 42 (1970): 348–62.

Couch, William, Jr. "Sinclair Lewis: Crisis in the American Dream." *CLA Journal* 7 (1964): 224–34.

Cowley, Malcolm, ed. *After the Genteel Tradition*. New York: Norton, 1937.

de Kruif, Paul. *The Sweeping Wind: A Memoir*. New York: Harcourt, Brace, Jovanovich, 1962.

DeVoto, Bernard. *The Literary Fallacy*. Boston: Little, Brown, 1944.

Dooley, David Joseph. *The Art of Sinclair Lewis*. Lincoln: University of Nebraska Press, 1967.

Fife, Jim L. "Two Views of the American West." *Western American Literature* 1 (1966): 34–43.

Flanagan, John T. "A Long Way to Gopher Prairie: Sinclair Lewis's Apprenticeship." *Southwest Review* 32 (1947): 403–13.

———. "The Minnesota Backgrounds of Sinclair Lewis's Fiction." *Minnesota History* 37 (March 1960): 1–13.

Fleissner, Robert F. "L'Affaire Sinclair Lewis: 'Anti-Semitism?' and Ancillary Matters." *Sinclair Lewis Newsletter* 4 (1972): 14–16.

———. " 'Something Out of Dickens' in Sinclair Lewis." *Bulletin of the New York Public Library* 74 (November 1970): 607–16.

Fleming, Robert E., and Esther Fleming. *Sinclair Lewis: A Reference Guide.* Boston: G. K. Hall, 1980.

French, Warren G., and Walter E. Kidd, eds. *American Winners of the Nobel Literary Prize.* Norman: University of Oklahoma Press, 1968.

Fyvel, T. R. "Martin Arrowsmith and His Habitat." *The New Republic* 18 (July 1955): 16–18.

Gardiner, Harold C., ed. *Fifty Years of the American Novel.* New York: Scribner's, 1952.

Gauss, Christian. "Sinclair Lewis vs. His Education." *The Saturday Evening Post* 26 December 1931.

Geismar, Maxwell. *American Moderns: From Rebellion to Conformity.* New York: Hill & Wang, 1958.

———. *The Last of the Provincials: The American Novel 1915–1925.* Boston: Houghton Mifflin, 1947.

Grebstein, Sheldon. "The Education of a Rebel: Sinclair Lewis at Yale." *New England Quarterly* 28 (September 1955): 377–82.

———. *Sinclair Lewis.* New York: Twayne, 1962.

———. "Sinclair Lewis and the Nobel Prize." *Western Humanities Review* 13 (1959): 163–71.

Griffin, Robert J., ed. *Twentieth Century Interpretations of* Arrowsmith. Englewood Cliffs, N.J.: Prentice-Hall, 1968.

Hague, John A. *American Character and Culture in a Changing World: Some Twentieth-Century Perspectives.* Westport, Conn.: Greenwood, 1979.

Hashisuchi, Yasuo. "*Arrowsmith* and Escapism." *Kyushu American Literature* 8 (1965): 14–18.

Hassan, Ihab. *Radical Innocence: The Contemporary American Novel.* Princeton: Princeton University Press, 1961.

Hilfer, Anthony Channell. *The Revolt from the Village.* Chapel Hill: University of North Carolina Press, 1969.

Hoffman, Frederick J. *The Twenties: American Writing in the Postwar Decade.* New York: Viking, 1955.

Hunt, Frazier. *One American and His Attempt at Education.* New York: Simon & Schuster, 1938.

Kazin, Alfred. *On Native Grounds: An Interpretation of Modern American Prose Literature.* New York: Harcourt, Brace & World, 1942.

Lea, James. "Sinclair Lewis and the Implied America." *Clio: An Interdisciplinary Journal* 3, no. 1 (1973): 21–34.

Light, Martin. "Lewis's Finicky Girls and Faithful Workers." *University of Kansas City Review* 30 (1963): 151–59.

———. *The Quixotic Vision of Sinclair Lewis.* West Lafayette, Ind.: Purdue University Press, 1975.

Love, Glen A. "New Pioneering on the Prairies: Nature, Progress, and the Individual in the Novels of Sinclair Lewis." *American Quarterly* 25 (1973): 55–77.

Lundquist, James. *Guide to Sinclair Lewis.* Columbus, Ohio: Merrill, 1971.

———. *Sinclair Lewis.* New York: Ungar, 1973.

Maddon, David, ed. *American Dreams and American Nightmares.* Carbondale: Southern Illinois University Press, 1970.

Manfred, Frederick F. "Sinclair Lewis: A Portrait." *American Scholar* 23 (1954): 162–84.

Millgate, Michael. *Amerian Social Fiction, James to Cozzens.* Edinburgh: Oliver & Boyd, 1964.

Neumann, Henry. "*Arrowsmith*: A Study in Vocational Ethics." *The American Review* 4 (March–April 1926): 245–54.

Oehlschlaeger, Fritz H. "Sinclair Lewis, Stuart Pratt Sherman, and the Writing of *Arrowsmith*." *Resources for American Literary Study* 9, no. 1 (1979): 24–30.

Schorer, Mark. *Sinclair Lewis.* Minneapolis: University of Minnesota Press, 1963.

———. *Sinclair Lewis: A Collection of Critical Essays.* Englewood Cliffs, N. J.: Prentice-Hall, 1962.

———. *Society and Self in the Novel.* English Institute Essays. New York: Columbia University Press, 1955.

Sinclair Lewis Newsletter. St. Cloud, Minn.: St. Cloud State College, 1969–.

Spitz, Leon. "Sinclair Lewis's Professor Gottlieb." *The American Hebrew* 158 (3 December 1948).

Stegner, Wallace, ed. *The American Novel.* New York: Basic Books, 1965.

Tepperman, Jay. "The Research Scientist in Modern Fiction." *Perspectives in Biology and Medicine* 3 (1960): 550–53.

Thorp, Willard. *American Writing in the Twentieth Century.* Cambridge: Harvard University Press, 1960.

Tuttleton, James W. *The Novel of Manners in America.* Chapel Hill: University of North Carolina Press, 1972.

Wagenaar, Dick. "The Knight and the Pioneer: Europe and America in the Fiction of Sinclair Lewis." *American Literature* 50 (1978): 230–49.

West, Rebecca. *The Strange Necessity.* New York: Doubleday, 1928.

Whipple, T. K. *Spokesmen: Modern Writers and American Life.* New York: Dutton, 1928.

Yoshida, Hiroshige. *A Sinclair Lewis Lexicon with a Critical Study of His Style and Method.* Tokyo: Hoyu Press, 1976.

Acknowledgments

"Sinclair Lewis and the Fortress of Reality" by Frederic I. Carpenter from *College English* 16, no. 7 (April 1955), © 1955 by the National Council of Teachers of English. Reprinted by permission of the publisher.

"Martin Arrowsmith: The Scientist as Hero" by Charles E. Rosenberg from *American Quarterly* 15, no. 3 (Fall 1963), © 1963 by the American Studies Association. Reprinted by permission of the author and *American Quarterly*.

"The Paper-Doll Characters of Sinclair Lewis's *Arrowsmith*" by Marilyn Morgan Helleberg from *The Mark Twain Journal* 14, no. 2 (Summer 1968), © 1968 by Thomas Penney. Reprinted by permission.

"*Arrowsmith:* Genesis, Development, Versions" by Lyon N. Richardson from *Twentieth Century Interpretations of* Arrowsmith, edited by Robert J. Griffin, © 1968 by Prentice-Hall, Inc. Reprinted by permission of Prentice-Hall, Inc., Englewood Cliffs, New Jersey. This essay originally appeared in *American Literature* 27 (May 1944), © 1955 by Duke University Press. Reprinted by permission.

"The Ambivalence towards Romance" (originally entitled "*Arrowsmith*: The Ambivalence towards Romance") by Martin Light from *The Quixotic Vision of Sinclair Lewis* by Martin Light, © 1975 Purdue University Press by Purdue Research Foundation, West Lafayette, Indiana 47907. Reprinted by permission.

"Three Max Gottliebs: Lewis's, Dreiser's, and Walker Percy's View of the Mechanist-Vitalist Controversy" by Mary G. Land from *Studies in the Novel* 15, no. 4 (Winter 1983), © 1983 by North Texas State University. Reprinted by permission.

"Sinclair Lewis, Max Gottlieb, and Sherlock Holmes" by Robert L. Coard from *Modern Fiction Studies* 31, no. 3 (Autumn 1985), © 1985 by Purdue Research Foundation, West Lafayette, Indiana 47907. Reprinted by permission.

Index